Praise for
Mere Anarchy

"Mr. Allen's writing has been this funny for fifty years. . . . He has sustained a writing style that remains impervious to the changing world around him. . . . *Mere Anarchy* is nostalgically enjoyable . . . timelessly bright."
—*The New York Times*

"Read every story in *Mere Anarchy*. . . . Like so much in Allen's unfailingly entertaining, mostly brilliant collections . . . at once painful, surreal, obsessive and, lest we forget, seriously funny."   —*Los Angeles Times Book Review*

"It goes without saying that Mr. Allen is a brilliant comic. . . . Enjoy the cream of what he's cooked up, and be grateful that he's [still] at it."   —*The New York Sun*

"Allen's ear for the pieties of language is sharp. . . . [He] is a supreme, devilish mimic."   —*The Hartford Courant*

"Allen remains pure, funny, and stubborn—the last feuilletoniste."   —*Paste*

"Delectable and often hilarious . . . wonderful . . . Find [*Mere Anarchy*]. It will be many eons before the expansion of the universe prevents [it] from being funny."
—*The Buffalo News*

"Allen piles the ludicrous on top of the ridiculous and tops it with an acidic lemon squeeze, and then just keeps the jokes coming."   —*Publishers Weekly*

MERE ANARCHY

WOODY ALLEN
MERE ANARCHY

RANDOM HOUSE TRADE PAPERBACKS
NEW YORK

Published in the United States by Random House Trade Paperbacks,
an imprint of The Random House Publishing Group,
a division of Random House, Inc., New York.

RANDOM HOUSE TRADE PAPERBACKS and colophon are trademarks of
Random House, Inc.

Originally published in hardcover in the United States by Random House,
an imprint of The Random House Publishing Group,
a division of Random House, Inc., in 2007.

The following essays first appeared in *The New Yorker*: "Caution, Falling
Moguls," "The Rejection," "Sing, Your Sacher Tortes," "On a Bad Day You
Can See Forever," "Attention Geniuses: Cash Only," Strung Out," "Above
the Law, Below the Box Springs," "Thus Ate Zarathustra," "Surprise
Rocks Disney Trial," and "Pinchuck's Law."

Grateful acknowledgement is made to *The New York Times* for permission
to reprint an extract from "India Jolted as One Legend Abducts Another"
by Celia W. Dugger (*The New York Times*, August 3, 2000),
copyright © 2000 by The New York Times Co., and an excerpt from
"The Year in Ideas: Enhanced Clothing" by Gina Bellafante
(*The New York Times Magazine*, December 15, 2002),
copyright © 2002 by Gina Bellafante. All rights reserved.
Reprinted by permission of *The New York Times*.

LIBRARY OF CONGRESS CATALOGING-IN-PUBLICATION DATA

Allen, Woody.
Mere anarchy / Woody Allen.
p. cm.
Collection of humorous pieces, many of which were originally published
in *The New Yorker*.
ISBN 978-0-8129-7950-3
I. Title.
PS3551.L44A6 2007
818'.5407—dc22   2006051880

Printed in the United States of America

www.atrandom.com

2 4 6 8 9 7 5 3 1

Book design by Simon M. Sullivan

CONTENTS

To Err Is Human—to Float, Divine 3

Tandoori Ransom 13

Sam, You Made the Pants Too Fragrant 25

This Nib for Hire 35

Calisthenics, Poison Ivy, Final Cut 45

Nanny Dearest 55

How Deadly Your Taste Buds, My Sweet 65

Glory Hallelujah, Sold! 73

Caution, Falling Moguls 81

The Rejection 93

Sing, You Sacher Tortes 99

On a Bad Day You Can See Forever 107

Attention Geniuses: Cash Only 117

Strung Out 127

Above the Law, Below the Box Springs 133

Thus Ate Zarathustra 141

Surprise Rocks Disney Trial 147

Pinchuck's Law 155

MERE ANARCHY

To Err Is Human—to Float, Divine

❧

G<small>ASPING FOR AIR</small>, my life passing before my eyes in a series of wistful vignettes, I found myself suffocating some months ago under the tsunami of junk mail that cascades through the slot in my door each morning after kippers. It was only our Wagnerian cleaning woman, Grendel, hearing a muffled falsetto from beneath myriad art-show invitations, charity squeezes, and pyrite contest jackpots I'd hit that extricated me with the help of our Bugsucker. As I was carefully filing the new postal arrivals alphabetically in the paper shredder, I noticed, amongst the profusion of catalogues that hawked everything from bird feeders to monthly deliveries of sundry drupe and hesperidium, there was an unsolicited little journal, banner-lined *Magical Blend*. Clearly aimed at the New Age market, its articles ranged in topic from crystal power to holistic healing and psychic vibrations, with tips on achieving spiritual energy, love versus stress, and exactly where to go and what forms to fill out to be reincarnated. The ads, which seemed scrupulously articulated to insulate against the unreasonableness of Bunco Squad malcontents, presented Therapeutic Ironisers, Vortex Water Energizers, and a product called Herbal Grobust designed to implement volumewise madam's Cavaillons. There was no shortage of psychic advice either, from sources such as the "spiritual intuitive" who double-checks her insights with "a consortium of angels named Consortium Seven," or a babe ecdysiastically christened Saleena, who offers to "balance your energy, awaken your DNA and attract abundance." Naturally, at the end of all these field trips to the center of the soul, a small emolument to cover stamps and any other expenses the guru may have incurred in another life is in order. The most startling persona of all, however, has to be the "founder and divine leader of the Hathor Ascension Movement on Planet Earth." Known to her followers as Gabrielle Hathor, a self-proclaimed goddess who is, according to her copywriter, "the fullness of source manifested in human form," this West Coast icon tells us, "There is a quickening of Karmic feedback. . . . Earth has entered a spiritual winter which will last 426,000 Earth years." Mindful of how rough a long winter can be, Ms. Hathor has started a movement to teach beings to ascend to "higher frequency dimensions," presumably where they can get out more and play a little golf.

"Levitation, instantaneous translocation, omniscience, ability to materialize and dematerialize and so on become part of one's normal abilities," the come-hither spiel lays on the unwary with a trowel, proclaiming that "from these higher frequency dimensions, the ascended being can perceive the lower frequencies while those on the lower frequencies cannot perceive the higher dimensions."

There is a fervid endorsement by someone named Pleiades MoonStar—a name that would cause no end of consternation for me if I were told at the last minute it belonged to my brain surgeon or pilot. Acolytes in Ms. Hathor's movement must submit to "a humiliating procedure" as part of a routine to dissolve their egos and get their frequencies jacked up. Actual cash payments are frowned upon, but for a little abject fealty and productive labor one can score a bed and a dish of organic mung beans while either gaining or losing consciousness.

I bring all this up because coincidentally, later that same day I was emerging from Hammacher Schlemmer, laid waste by obsessive indecision over whether to buy a computerized duck press or the world's finest portable guillotine, when I bumped like the *Titanic* into an old iceberg I had known in college, Max Endorphine. Plump in midlife, with the eyes of a cod and sporting a toupee upholstered with sufficient pile to create a trompe l'oeil pompadour, he pumped my hand and launched into tales of his recent good fortune.

"What can I tell you, boychick, I hit it big. Got in touch with my inner spiritual self, and from there on it was Fat City."

"Can you elaborate?" I queried, registering for the first time his natty bespoke ensemble and advanced-tumor-sized pinkie ring.

"I guess I shouldn't really be jawing with someone on a lower frequency, but since we go way back—"

"Frequency?"

"I'm talking dimensions. Those of us in the upper octaves are taught not to squander healthy ions on mortal troglodytes of which you qualify—no offense. Not that we don't study and appreciate the lower forms—thanks to Leeuwenhoek, if you get my meaning." Suddenly, with a falcon's instinct for prey, Endorphine turned his head toward a long-legged blonde in a micro-miniskirt straining to locate a taxi.

"Clock the apparition with the state-of-the-art pout," he said, his salivary glands shifting into third.

"Must be a centerfold," I piped, feeling the sudden onset of heatstroke, "judging from her see-through blouse."

"Watch this," Endorphine said, whereupon he took a deep breath and began rising off the ground. To the amazement of both myself and Miss July, he was levitating a foot above Fifty-seventh Street in front of Hammacher Schlemmer. Searching for wires, the sweet young thing brought her show closer.

"Hey, how do you do that?" she purred.

"Here. Here's my address," Endorphine said. "I'll be home tonight after eight. Drop by. I'll have you off your feet in no time."

"I'll bring the Petrus," she cooed, stuffing the logistics of their rendezvous into the abyss of her cleavage, and wiggled off as Endorphine slowly descended to ground level.

"What gives?" I said. "Are you Houdini?"

"Oh, well," he sighed benevolently, "since I'm deigning to converse with practically a paramecium, I may as well give you the whole schmear. Let's repair to the Stage Deli and decimate some schnecken while I hold court." With that there was an audible pop and Endorphine vanished. I sucked in my breath and clasped my hand to my open mouth like a startled Gish sister. Seconds later he reappeared, contrite.

"Sorry. I forgot you bottom-feeders can't dematerialize and translocate. My error. Let's just hoof it." I was still pinching myself when Endorphine began his tale.

"OK," he said. "Flashback six months prior, when Mrs. Endorphine's little boy Max was at emotional ducks and drakes over a series of tribulations, which, if you count my misplaced beret, topped Job's. First, this fortune cookie from Taiwan I was tutoring in anatomical hydraulics eighty-sixes me for an apprentice pie maker, then I get sued to the tune of many dead presidents for backing my Jaguar through a Christian Science Reading Room. Add to that my one son from a previous connubial holocaust gives up his lucrative law practice to become a ventriloquist. So here I am, blue and funky, scouring the town for a raison d'être, a spiritual center as it were, when suddenly, out of the ether, I come across this ad in the latest issue of *Vibes Illustrated*. A spa type of joint that liposuctions off your bad karma, raising you to a higher frequency wherein you can at last hold sway over nature à la Faust. As a rule I'm too savvy to bite on a scam like that, but when I dig the CEO is an actual goddess in human form, I figure what could be bad? And there's no charge. They don't take dough. The system's based on some variation of slavery, but in return you get these crystals, which empower you, and all the Saint-John's-wort you can scarf up. Oh, I'm leaving out she humiliates you. But it's part of the therapy. So her minions frenched my bed and affixed an ass's tail to the back of my trousers unbeknownst to me. Sure I was a laughingstock for a while, but let me tell you, it dissolved my ego. Suddenly I realized I had lived in previous lives—first as a simple burgomaster and then as Lucas Cranach the Elder . . . or no, I forget, maybe it was the kid. Anyhow, the next thing I know, I wake up on my crude pallet and my frequency is in the stratosphere. I got like this nimbus around my occiput and I'm omniscient. I mean right off I hit the double at Belmont and within a week I draw crowds every time I show up at the Bellagio in Vegas. If I'm ever unsure about a nag or whether to hit or stick at blackjack, there's this consortium of angels I tap into. I mean, just 'cause someone's got wings and is made of ectoplasm don't mean they can't handicap. Clock this wad."

Endorphine extracted several bale-sized bundles of thousand-dollar bills from each pocket.

"Oops, excuse me," he said, fumbling to retrieve some rubies that had fallen out of his jacket when he produced the cornucopia of greenbacks.

"And she doesn't take any remuneration for this service?" I inquired, my heart taking wing like a peregrine falcon.

"Well, you know, that's how it is with avatars. They're all big sports."

That night, despite a welter of imprecations from the distaff side plus a quick call by her to the firm of Shmeikel and Sons to check if our pre-nup covered the sudden onset of dementia praecox, I found myself skying west to the Sublime Ascension Center with its divinity in residence, a vision in Frederick's of Hollywood named Galaxie Sunstroke. Bidding me enter the shrine that dominated her compound, an abandoned farm curiously resembling the Spahn ranch of Manson lore, she put down her emery board and got comfortable on a divan.

"Take a load off your feet, honey," she said to me in tones less Martha Graham than Iris Adrian. "So, you want to get in touch with your spiritual center."

"Yes. I'd like my frequency turned up, the ability to levitate, translocate, dematerialize, and sufficient omniscience to divine in advance the randomly selected numerals that comprise the New York State Lottery."

"What do you do for a living?" she inquired, oddly unomniscient for a creature of her reputed majesty.

"Night watchman at a wax museum," I replied, "but it's not as fulfilling as it sounds."

Turning to one of the Nubians who fanned her with palm fronds, she said, "What do you think, boys? He looks like he'd make a good groundskeeper. Maybe take care of the septic tank."

"Thank you," I said as I knelt, pressing my face to the ground in abasement.

"OK," she said, clapping her hands as a quincunx of loyal minions scurried forward from behind beaded curtains. "Give him a rice bowl and shave his head. Till a bed opens up he can sleep with the chickens."

"I hear and obey," I murmured, averting my eyes lest a direct look at Ms. Sunstroke could distract her from the crossword puzzle she had begun. With that I was hurried away, slightly apprehensive with the thought that I might be branded.

As far as I could discern in the days following, the compound was awash with losers of every description: poltroons and nudniks, actresses who guided their each move by the planets, the overweight, a man who had been involved in some kind of taxidermy scandal, a midget in denial. All sought to ascend to a higher plane while they labored around the clock in lobotomized submission to the supreme goddess, who occasionally was seen on the grounds dancing like Isadora Duncan or inhaling from a long pipe and then laughing like Seabiscuit. In return for a few spells and passes now and then from the compound's chief shaman, an ex-bouncer I thought I recognized from a documentary on Megan's Law, the faithful were expected to toil twelve to sixteen hours a day harvesting fruits and vegetables for the staff to consume and to manufacture assorted salable commodities such as nude playing cards, foam-rubber dashboard dice, and restaurant crumbers. In addition to my responsibilities maintaining the drainage system, as groundskeeper I was expected to spear and bag the discarded carob-bar wrappers and cigarette papers that dotted the landscape. The daily fare, which leaned heavily on alfalfa seeds, miso, and ionized water, was a little difficult to get used to, but a sawbuck laid on one of the less committed lamas whose brother ran a nearby diner secured an intermittent tuna melt. Discipline was lax and one was expected to act responsibly, although breaking the dietary rules or shirking on the job could lead to a flogging or being hooked up to a field telephone. Humiliation followed humiliation as part of an ego-cleansing ritual, and finally when it was decreed that I was to make love to a karmic priestess who was a dead ringer for Bill Parcells, I decided it was time to pack it in. Inching on my back underneath the barbed-wire fence, I lit out in the dead of night and flagged down the last 747 to the Upper West Side.

"So," my wife said, with the benign tolerance of one addressing the prematurely senile, "did you dematerialize and translocate here, or is that a Continental Airlines cocktail napkin I see dangling from your collar?"

"I didn't stay long enough for that," I parried, fuming at her subtle contumely, "but I sweated enough to pick up *this* little tour de force." And with that I levitated six inches off the floor and hovered while her mouth spread like the shark's in *Jaws*.

"You lower-frequency know-it-alls just don't get it," I said, rubbing it in to her with unrestrained glee yet forgivingly. The woman let out a piercing shriek of the type that alerts to enemy bombardment and bid our children run and take refuge from this nightmarish voodoo. It was at this moment I began to realize I couldn't get down, and try as I might to de-elevate, I found the maneuver impossible. Pandemonium akin to the stateroom scene in *A Night at the Opera* ensued, the children shaking and bellowing hysterically as neighbors ran in to save us from what must have sounded like a bloodbath. All the while I strained mightily to lower myself, grimacing and twisting like a mime. Finally, leaping into action, the better half took it upon herself to master this warp in conventional physics by procuring a neighbor's ski, which she brought down hard on the top of my head, sending me earthbound in a thrice.

The last I heard, Max Endorphine had dematerialized never to rematerialize again. As far as Galaxie Sunstroke and her Sublime Ascension Center, rumor has it they were dismantled by Treasury agents and reincarnated, or was it reincarcerated? As for me, I never was able to gain loft again or guess in advance the name of a single horse at Aqueduct that would run better than sixth.

TANDOORI RANSOM

The legendary outlaw Veerappan, a lean man with a twirling, jet black mustache, has ranged through the jungles of South India for a generation. . . . Mr. Veerappan stands accused of 141 murders. . . . On Sunday he put into action what the police are calling his boldest, most diabolical plan. . . . He abducted Rajkumar, 72, a beloved movie star whose half-century-long career portraying Hindu gods, kings of yore and heroes of every kind has endowed him with a mystical stature of his own.

—*The New York Times*, August 3, 2000

O THESPIS, MY MUSE, my blessing, my curse! Like you I have been graced by the gods with a vivid and abundant gift for the performing arts. A born talent with heroic lineaments, the aquiline profile of a Barrymore, and the corybantic suppleness of a strutter and fretter in the Kabuki, I was not content to settle merely for the bounteous hand dealt me by providence but immersed myself assiduously in the dramatic arts of classical theater, of dance and mime. It has been said that I can do more with the raising of an eyebrow than most actors can do with their entire bodies. To this day, denizens of the Neighborhood Playhouse recount in hushed tones the psychological detail with which I imbued Parson Manders during a summer workshop. The downside of a histrionic life is that beneath a certain minimum figure, the number of calories required each day to postpone starvation demands that I bus the tables at Taco-Pox, a burrito palace that languishes before the unsuspecting on La Cienega Boulevard like a Venus flytrap. That's why when I received a message on my PhoneMate from Pontius Perry, the high-powered agent at Career Busters, Hollywood's hottest talent emporium, I sensed that maybe it was finally my time to taste a little back end. This notion was reinforced when Perry told me I could use the private elevator reserved for top box-office draws and wouldn't have to put my lungs at risk inhaling next to a supporting player. I divined that the business at hand just might revolve around the bestselling novel *Row Mutant, Row,* in which the role of Josh Airhead was coveted by every male star in SAG. I was perfect for the tragic intellectual, possessing just the right admixture of nobility and sangfroid.

"I think I got something for you, kid," Pontius Perry told me as I faced him in his office, which had been decorated by two *très chic* new Hollywood designers in a combination of postmodern and Visigoth.

"If it's the part of Josh Airhead, I want the director to know I'll be using a prosthesis. I see him with a miser's hump, embittered from years of rejection and perhaps even with some layered wattles."

"Actually, they're talking to Dustin about Airhead. No, this is a whole nother project. It's a thriller about some wino who looks to boost a moonstone-type rock from betwixt the eyes of a Buddha or some such idol of that nature. I only gave the script a perfunctory read, but I managed to glom sufficient gist before merciful Morpheus did a number on me."

"I see, so I play a soldier of fortune. A role that gives me a chance to utilize some of my old gymnastic training. All those classes in theatrical swordplay stand poised to bear fruit."

"Let me level with you, boychick," Perry said, peering out the six-foot picture window at the molasses-colored smog that the citizens of Los Angeles favor over actual air. "Harvey Afflatus is playing the lead."

"Oh, then they see me in a character role—the hero's best friend, a trusted confidant who propels the plot from within."

"Er, not exactly. See, Afflatus needs a lighting double."

"A what?"

"Someone to stand on a mark for the tedious hours it takes the cameraman to light the scene, someone who vaguely resembles the star so the lamps and shadows won't be too far out of whack. Then, at the last second, when they're ready to call action and make the shot, the zombie—er, the double—takes a hike and the money comes on and plays the part."

"But why me?" I asked. "Do they really need an actor of genius for that?"

" 'Cause you vaguely resemble Afflatus—oh, you'll never be in his class lookswise, but the morphology meshes."

"I'd have to think about it," I said. "I am up for the voice of Waffles in a puppet rendition of *Uncle Vanya*."

"Think quick," Perry said. "The plane leaves for Thiruvananthapuram in two hours. It's better than minesweeping the used enchiladas off the tabletops in some Tex-Mex tamale factory. Who knows, you could get discovered."

TEN HOURS LATER, after a delay on the runway while the flight crew turned the aircraft upside down to retrieve an escaped cobra, I found myself skying toward India. The producer of the film, Hal Roachpaste, had explained to me that due to the last-minute decision of the leading lady to bring her rottweiler along there would not be room for me on the charter flight, and so they had booked me passage as an untouchable with Bandhani Air, India's equivalent of Crazy Eddie. Fortunately there was room for me aboard a return flight carrying a convention of beggars, and though I couldn't parse a word of Urdu I was fascinated as they compared afflictions and examined one another's bowls.

The trip was uneventful save for some "light chop," which caused the passengers to ricochet off the cabin wall like boiled atoms. By dawn's early light we deplaned at a makeshift airstrip in Bhubaneshwar. From there it was a bit of a jaunt by steam train to Ichalkaranji, on to Omkareshwar by tongas, and we finally arrived at the location in Jhalawar via *dhooli*. I was given a hearty welcome by the crew and told not to unpack but to go stand directly on my mark so lighting could begin lest we fall behind our schedule. A consummate profes-sional, I assumed my place on a hill in the noonday heat and did yeoman's work, buckling only with the onset of sunstroke at teatime.

The first week of filming passed with predictable mood swings. The director, it turned out, was a spineless yes-man who repeated every utterance Afflatus made, deeming each worthy of inclusion in the works of Aristotle. In my opinion Afflatus had missed the central core of the lead character and rather than risk audience displeasure by giving Colonel But-terfat the dimension of self-doubt, he changed his profession from colonel in the military to Kentucky colonel, owner and breeder of Thoroughbreds. How he won the Preakness in the Vale of Kashmir puzzled me and apparently disconcerted the writer too, whose belt and necktie had to be taken from him. As acting is 90 percent voice, I must add here that Afflatus is cursed with an adenoidal whine that hatches in the throat and reverberates off his septum like a kazoo. I tried speaking to him during a break about some ways I thought he could flesh out his character, but it was too radical a shift in concentra-tion from the book that he had vowed would teach him all about Smurfs before the end of shooting. In the evenings it was my habit to keep to myself, dining at a café on murg and chai, though in my third week I miscalculated the sincerity of one of the comely locals who answered to Shakira and in true Indian fashion embraced me with her two arms while the other four rifled through my pants.

Midway through the filming is when everything hit the fan.

We had finally gotten over the internecine clashes of temperament, including the hiding of Hal Roachpaste's blood thinner by the author, and the project had begun to sprout wings. A rumor came back that the dailies were good, and Babe Roachpaste, the producer's wife, claimed the footage she had seen rivaled *Citizen Kane*. Seized by manic euphoria, Afflatus suggested it might be time to begin planning an Oscar campaign and lobbied for a flack to ghostwrite his acceptance speech.

I remember standing on my mark as usual, trying to give the cameraman a target to line up on, my face held high, jaw jutting out at much the same angle Afflatus's does, when from out of left field emerges an exultation of rag-heads who charge the set screaming like Apaches. They coldcock the director with an ashtray lifted from the Bombay Hilton and scatter the panic-stricken crew. Next thing I know, there's a bag over my head, which is then adroitly knotted, and I'm being carted off in a fireman's carry. As the martial arts were part of my acting background, I suddenly snapped to the ground and uncoiled, sending forth a lightning-power kick, which fortunately for my abductors hit air and caused me to fall directly into the open trunk of a waiting Plymouth, where the door was promptly locked. The combination of the fierce Indian heat and the force with which I hit my head on a purloined elephant's tusk in the boot of the van knocked me senseless. I came to sometime later in an inky black void as the vehicle bumped and rumbled over the jagged terrain of what must have been a mountain road. Using deep-breathing exercises that I had mastered in acting class, I managed to retain my composure for at least eight seconds before emitting a medley of bloodcurdling bleats and hyperventilated into oblivion. I dimly recall the bag being removed from my head in the mountaintop cave of a wild-eyed bandit chieftain with a twirling jet-black mustache and the psychotic intensity of Eduardo Ciannelli in *Gunga Din*. Brandishing a scimitar, he had apparently gone ballistic over some shoddy abduction work by his trio of simpering myrmidons.

"Worms, vermin, beetles! I send you out to snatch a cinema luminary, and this is what you bring me?" the hash-high CEO ranted, nostrils flaring like sails that had caught the wind.

"Master, I beg you," groveled the Dalit hailed as Abu.

"A stand-in, a supernumerary not even—a lighting double," the *grand fromage* bellowed.

"But you will agree there's a resemblance, master?" squeaked one trembling plaintiff.

"Crab! Lizard! You're telling me this midden of offal could be mistaken for Harvey Afflatus? It's like comparing gold and mud."

"But exalted one, they hired him exactly because—"

"Silence, or I'll cut your tongue out. I'm looking here to score for maybe fifty or a hundred large, and you deliver up this zero-talent potzer whom I guarantee, or my name's not Veerappan, will not fetch a lead rupee."

So this was he, the legendary brigand I had read about. A master at cruelty perhaps, and quick to slaughter, but clearly a philistine when it came to evaluating talent.

"I'm sure, sire, we can get *something* for him. The production won't just walk if we threaten to dismember one of their own. True, we've all heard tales of the major studios not returning phone calls, but if we send back an organ at a time—"

"Enough, you slimy jellyfish," the evil dacoit leader hissed. "Afflatus is currently running very hot. He's coming off two features that did solid business even in the smaller markets. For the rodent we've got stashed we'd be lucky to make back our chickpea nut."

"I'm sorry, magnificent one," wept Veerappan's errant minion. "It's just that when the light hits him a certain way, his face exhibits the basic contours of said movie idol."

"Can't you see he lacks all charisma? There's a reason that Afflatus sets marks in places like Boise and Yuma. It's called star stature. This trombenik is the type that drives a cab or works at an answering service waiting for that one big break that never comes."

"Now, just a minute," I yelled, despite eight inches of black masking tape across my mouth, but before I could really warm to my theme I received a wallop in the sconce with a *huqqa*. I held my tongue as Veerappan segued into his peroration. All the crass bunglers were to be decapitated, he decreed benevolently. As for me, the group treasurer suggested they lower the ransom demand, give it a few days, and see if the production ponied up. If not, their plan was to purée me. Knowing what I did of Hal Roachpaste, I had complete confidence that the company had already contacted the U.S. embassy and would of course accede to the bandit's most extravagant demands rather than see a colleague mistreated in any way. After five days of no response, however, in which Veerappan's spies told him the writer had reworked the script and the film had pulled up stakes and relocated in Auckland, I began to feel uneasy. Word was that Roachpaste had not wanted to bother the Indian government with a complaint but had vowed as he blew town to do all in his power to free me short of paying a cent in ransom, which he felt could set an awkward precedent. When news of my plight appeared as a filler in the rear pages of *Backstage,* a group of politically active extras deemed it an outrage and swore to hold a midnight vigil but could not jimmy loose sufficient capital to purchase the required candles.

So, how is it that I'm here to tell the story given Veerappan's deadline and lust for my carcass? Because with three hours left to go and a roomful of frenzied fanatics honing their krises and diagramming my body on a chart, I was suddenly awakened in my ropes by a pair of swarthy eyes peering out from between a turban and a burnoose.

"Quick, kid, don't scream," the intruder whispered in tones more consistent with Greenpoint than Bhopal.

"Who's that?" I said, my senses numbed from a scant diet of *aloo* and *tarka dal.*

"Quick, doff these togs and walk with me. And keep calm—the place is awash with humanity's dregs."

"Absolutely," I yelped, recognizing the voice of my agent, Pontius Perry.

"Let's shake it. We got time for amenities at Nate'n Al's tomorrow."

And so, under the crafty guidance of my professional representative, I was sprung from inevitable dissection by Veerappan, titan of rogues.

At Nate'n Al's the next day Perry explained over a panoply of derma that he had heard about my straits at a seder at Mr. Chow's.

"The whole thing really stuck in my craw, and then I remembered when I was younger and used to put on one of those penny cardboard mustaches, all the kids in school would rib me over my uncanny resemblance to His Exalted Highness the Nizam of Hyderabad. Once that lightbulb went off, the rest was a piece of chocolate layer. I mean, sure, I had to do some fast talking because the nizam's been extinct for lo these many years, but I'm an agent and fast talking's how I set my table."

"But why would you risk your life for me?" I queried, detecting the faint aroma of fish five days old in his spiel.

"Only 'cause in your absence I got you the lead in a feature. Heavy scratch. It's a drug-war flick. All to be shot in the jungles of Colombia. Anti-Medellín. I guess that's why some of the death squads took a blood oath to waste a few cast members if a film does come down there, but the director waves it off as saber rattling. I can't believe how many actors passed, but that only helped me jack up the lolly for you. Hey, where you going?"

Outside in the smog where I had vanished like a cat, I ran

to buy a newspaper and check the want ads. Maybe there was an opening for a cabdriver or answering-service operator like Veerappan had suggested. Of course Pontius Perry's 10 percent would be a lot less, but at least he wouldn't have to ever wake up and find my ear in his FedEx.

SAM, YOU MADE THE PANTS
TOO FRAGRANT

❧

A company named Foster-Miller, for instance, recently designed a textile with conductive properties: each thread can transmit electrical currents . . . so that Americans will one day . . . be able to recharge their cellphones with their polo shirts. . . . Technologically Enabled Clothing . . . has developed [a vest that conceals] . . . a "hydration system," a back pocket for a water bottle with a straw running through the vest's collar to the wearer's mouth. . . .

Next year DuPont will introduce a fabric that can temporarily imprison offensive scents—so that, say, a shirt that spent the night in a smoke-filled bar will arrive home at 5 a.m. smelling as if it passed the hours in a spring meadow. DuPont's scientists have also developed Teflon-treated fabric; spills bounce right off.

The South Korean company Kolon, in turn, has developed the "fragrant suit," treated with anxiety-soothing herbs.

—*The New York Times Magazine*, December 15, 2002

RAN INTO REG MILLIPEDE sometime back. Reg's a gaming crony from those piping times in Jolly Old when I stood as poetry editor of *Dry Heaves: A Journal of*

Opinion. If the truth be known, the two of us gave as good as we got over whist and rummy at the Pair of Shoes or Lord Curzon's Club on the street that bears his name.

"I get to your city now and again," Milliepede acknowledged as we stood on the corner of Park and Seventy-fourth. "Mostly on business. I'm vice president in charge of customer relations for one of the biggest charnel houses on the Isle of Wight."

I'd venture we swapped mellow souvenirs for the better part of an hour, during which time I couldn't help noticing that my companion would sporadically tilt his face down and left, seemingly to siphon some beverage from what appeared to be a spigot discreetly camouflaged beneath the underside of his lapel.

"Are you all right?" I finally asked, half expecting the details of some unspeakable accident that culminated in a newfangled ambulatory IV. "Are you on some kind of drip?"

"You mean this?" Milliepede said, pointing toward his breast pocket. "Aha—you observant rascal. No, this is merely a masterpiece of engineering slash tailoring. You're undoubtedly up on how the entire medical profession is suddenly bonkers about drinking lots of water. Seems it flushes out the kidneys, along with myriad ancillary benefits. Well, this tropical worsted has its own built-in hydration system. There's a storage tank in the left trouser leg with a series of pipes that run around the waist and up to a faucet tactfully hemmed into the shoulder pad. I have a digital computer stitched against my inseam that enables me to activate a pump just behind some pleats that forces Evian through this fiber-optic straw. Because of its ingenious cut I still manage to maintain a dapper line. I'm sure you'll agree the garment speaks for breeding."

Examining Millipede's suit with an incredulity usually reserved for UFO sightings, I had to admit it smacked of the miraculous.

"There's this perfectly marvelous tailoring establishment on Savile Row," he said, pressing its address into my palm. "Bandersnatch and Bushelman. Postmodern fabrics. I guarantee you'll want to revamp your entire wardrobe—which mightn't be a bad idea judging from that threadbare tribute to Emmett Kelly you're currently sporting. Be sure and tell them I sent you round, and ask for Binky Peplum. He'll do right by your pocketbook. Ta."

While I pretended, for old times' sake, to double up at Millipede's Emmett Kelly slander, I wanted to impale him on a pike. His invidious comparison with the clown's attire lodged in my bosom like a scorpion's tail, and I resolved to invest in a bespoke ensemble the moment my frequent-flier miles swelled to underwrite a trip abroad. The dream became a reality at summer's end when I at last entered the high-tech portals of Bandersnatch and Bushelman on Savile Row, where either the salesman or a praying mantis in gabardine eyeballed me like I was being cultured in a petri dish.

"One of them's wandered in again," he yelled to a colleague. "If I stand you to half a guinea," he said to me in a voice reeking of the judicial bench, "how can I be sure you'll buy a bowl of soup and not squander it on lager?"

"I'm a customer," I squealed, reddening. "I've traveled from America to refresh my wardrobe. Reg Millipede's chum. He said to keep a keen eye out for Mr. Binky Peplum."

"Aha," replied the seller, checking for the precise location of my jugular. "Look no further. Now that you mention it, I do recall Millipede warning us someone of your stripe might be stopping by. Yes, he spoke of you—total absence of any flair . . . child of a lesser god . . . it's all coming back to me."

"Certainly my goal has never been to play the fop," I explained. "I'm here simply to be measured for a sensible outfit."

"Are you interested in any special aromas?" Peplum asked, pulling out his order pad and winking at an associate.

"Aromas? No, just a classic blue three-button, conservatively cut. Perhaps even a few shirts. I had envisioned Sea Island cotton if it's not too dear. Although now that you bring it up, I do detect the faint scent of frankincense and myrrh."

"That's my suit," Peplum confessed. "Our new line offers a wide variety of odors. Night-blooming jasmine, attar of roses, balsam of Mecca. Come here, Ramsbottom." Another salesman darted over as if waiting to be cued. "Ramsbottom is wearing freshly baked rolls—the aroma, that is."

I leaned in to sample the delicious smell of oven-baked bread. "Very tasty suit. I mean it's a lovely mohair," I said.

"We can imbue your raiments with any fragrance from

patchouli to twice-cooked pork. That will be all, Ramsbottom."

"I just want a simple blue suit. Although I've toyed with gray flannel," I chuckled with an impish grin.

"Here at Bandersnatch and Bushelman we're not about simple fabrics," Peplum said, leaning in to me conspiratorially. "I beg you, don't hang back with the brutes." Taking down a natty pin-striped jacket from the store dummy, Peplum offered it up to me.

"Look here, try and stain it," he said.

"Stain the jacket?" I asked.

"Yes. I'm sure, even knowing you so little as I do, you're a man who deposits a vast amount of ichor on your clothing. You know, butterfat, Elmer's glue, chocolate creams, cheap red wine, ketchup. Have I captured you accurately?"

"I guess I'm as prone to soiling a garment as the next man," I stammered.

"Depends how slovenly the next man is," chirped Peplum. "Let me provide some samples for you to try." He handed me a combination plate with assorted sauces and ointments, each life-threatening to fabric.

"You really want me to?"

"Yes, yes—spread some blackberry currant on the jacket, or the Fox's U-Bet syrup." Summoning the courage to defy years of social conditioning, I ladled on a dollop of axle grease only to find that it could not be made to stick or leave its trace. This held true for soot and tomato juice, toothpaste and India ink.

"See the difference when I apply these same substances to your clothing," Peplum said, shaking a generous portion of A.1. sauce on my trousers. "Note how it actually discolors the material permanently."

"I see, I see, yes, it's horrendous," I said, stricken.

"Good choice of words," Peplum chortled. "Ruined forever, and yet for a few hundred quid extra, you'll never have to think bib or consort with common dry cleaners again. Or let's say the wee ones finger paint on your vicuña sports coat."

"I don't want a vicuña sports coat," I explained, "and rather than get too pricey, I prefer to take my chances with a little naphtha."

"By the way," Peplum noted, "we also have a fabric that will reject any odor. I mean, I don't know what your wife's like, but I can just imagine."

"She's a very handsome woman," I quickly said.

"Well, you know, it's all relative. I might look at the same face and see something you'd find for sale in a live-bait store."

"Now, just a minute," I protested.

"I'm just theorizing. I mean, let's say you have a receptionist with a rear end you can't keep your eyes off, long, tan legs, ample cleavage, and a pout—plus she's always running her tongue over her lips. Get the picture, friend?"

"Perhaps I'm obtuse," I said weakly.

"Perhaps? Let me limn it more graphically, pilgrim. Let's just say you're bouncing this little slab of cheesecake at every motel in the tristate area."

"I'd never—"

"Please. Your secret's safe with me. Now, you come home and the ball and chain perceives the subtlest trace of Quelques Fleurs on your tattersall vest. Starting to have the epiphany? Next thing you know, either you're sweating to keep out of alimony jail or the immortal beloved goes ballistic and you wind up like one of those old Weegee photos with a suppurating excavation between the orbs."

"This is not a real problem for me," I said. "I just want something relaxed but elegant to wear on special occasions."

"Sure you do—but with an eye to the future. We don't just make suits, we clothe our customers in a postmodern environment. What do you do, Mr.—?"

"Duckworth, Benno Duckworth. Perhaps you've read my volume on anapestic dimeter."

"Can't say I have," Peplum said. "But you impress me as the mercurial type. Moody. I'd venture even bipolar. Silly to deny it. I can see even in the brief time we've spent together how your psyche oscillates from benign and avuncular to frazzled or, if the right buttons were pushed, homicidal."

"I assure you, Mr. Peplum, I'm stable. My hands may be shaking now, but it's because all I want is a blue suit—not an environment. Just something that suggests accomplishment yet is understated."

"And here I have exactly the item. A fine Scotch wool. But loomed with our own secret cocktail of mood elevators to provide you with a constant sense of well-being."

"Unmotivated well-being," I snapped with emerging sarcasm in my voice.

"Well, it's motivated by the suit. Let's say you lost your wallet with all your credit cards and you get home and the little kumquat's totaled the Lamborghini plus you find a ransom note demanding eight times your net worth if you ever want to lay eyes on your kids again. With this garment on your back you never lose your good humor or affable manner. The truth is, you actually enjoy your plight."

"And the children?" I asked, terrified. "Where are they? Bound and gagged in some basement?"

"It won't be as it appears now—not while you're caressed by one of our antidepressant textiles."

"Right," I parried, "but when I take off the suit, won't I experience withdrawal symptoms?"

"Er, well, there are some weak sisters who tend to become more introverted once the jacket's been removed. Why? Would you ever contemplate ending it all?"

"Yes, well," I said, backing toward the fire exit, "speaking of ending it all, I must go. I have a pet raccoon home that needs milking." As the fingers in my pocket closed around my pepper spray should any attempt to hamper egress be made, my attention was caught by a stunning navy swatch that Peplum had not yet presented.

"Oh, this," Peplum described when I queried him on it. "The threads are interwoven with thousands of conductive wires. The garment not only drapes beautifully but will recharge your cellular phone when you rub the instrument on your sleeve before placing a call."

"Now, that's more like it," I said, envisioning the finished product to be at once stylish yet practical while announcing indirectly to my peers that I was indeed a member of the avant-garde. Peplum, seeing that he had hit pay dirt, pulled out a purchase order and moved in on me to close the deal with the lethal economy of Philidor's mate. As I pulled out a check and accepted his Mont Blanc, my heart racing with the promise of this sartorial coup, it was none other than Ramsbottom, his face drained of all color, who came bolting in from the other room.

"Problems, Binky," he whispered.

"You're ashen," Peplum said.

"Our cellular recharging suit," Ramsbottom bleated, "the one we sold yesterday—remember?—cashmere with microscopic conductive wires. You know, the kind you can just rub your cell phone on to get it juiced."

"Not now," Peplum said, coughing. "I've a, you know," he said, rolling his eyes toward me.

"Huh?" Ramsbottom murmured.

"You know, there's one born every minute," Peplum shot back.

"Oh, yes, sure," the nervous cohort chattered. "It's just that the bloke who put on the cell-phone-charging suit stepped out of our showroom, touched the handle of his car, and ricocheted off Buckingham Palace. He's in intensive care."

"Hmm," Peplum mused, rapidly computing every possible liability. "Probably didn't realize it's fatal to make contact with metal while you're thusly clad. Oh, well, you notify his family, I'll give a heads-up to legal. That's the fourth time this month a conductive-suit customer has had to go on life support. Now, where was I? Oh yes, Ducksauce? Duckbill? Where'd he go?"

Let him try and find me. High voltage in a pair of pants is exactly the kind of thing that sends me ricocheting directly to Barneys, where I bought a marked-down three-button job off the peg, and it doesn't do anything postmodern unless you count picking up lint.

THIS NIB FOR HIRE

❧

It is said Dostoyevsky wrote for money to sponsor his lust for the roulette tables of St. Petersburg. Faulkner and Fitzgerald too leased their gifts to ex-schmatte moguls who stacked the Garden of Allah with scriveners brought west to spitball box-office reveries. Apocryphal or not, the mollifying lore of geniuses who temporarily mortgaged their integrity gamboled around my cortex some months ago when the phone rang as I was adrift in my apartment trying to tickle from my muse a worthy theme for that big book I must one day write.

"Mealworm?" the voice on the other end barked through lips clearly enveloping a panatela.

"Yes, this is Flanders Mealworm. Who's calling?"

"E. Coli Biggs. Name mean anything to you?"

"Er, can't say it actually—"

"No matter. I'm a film producer—and a big one. Christ, don't you read *Variety*? I got the number one grosser in Guinea-Bissau."

"The truth is I'm more conversant with the literary land-scape," I confessed.

"Yeah, I know. I read *The Hockfleisch Chronicles*. That's on account of why I want we have a sit-down. Be at the Carlyle Hotel three-thirty today. Royal Suite. I'm staying under the name of Ozymandias Hoon to stave off the local wannabes from inundating me with scripts."

"How did you get my number?" I inquired. "It's unlisted."

"From the Internet. It's there alongside the X-rays of your colonoscopy. Just materialize on cue, skeezix, and pretty soon we'll both be able to ladle beaucoup skins into our respective Marmites." With that he slammed the receiver into its cradle with sufficient velocity to buckle my eustachian tube.

It was not unthinkable that the name E. Coli Biggs would mean zilch to me. As I had made clear, my existence was not the glitzy whirlwind of film festivals and starlets but the Spartan regimen of the dedicated bard. Over the years I had churned out several unpublished novels on lofty philosophical themes before finally being given a first printing by Shlock House. My book, in which a man travels back in time and hides King George's wig, thus hastening the Stamp Act, obviously ruffled establishment feathers with its bite. Still, I regarded myself as an emerging and uncompromising talent, and mulling over Biggs's command to heel at the Carlyle made me chary of selling out to some philistine Hollywood platypus. The idea that he might fantasize renting my inspiration to pen a screenplay at once disgusted me and piqued my ego. After all, if the progenitors of *The Great Gatsby* and *The*

Sound and the Fury could warm their stoves courtesy of some prestige-hungry West Coast suits, why not Mrs. Mealworm's little bunting? I was supremely confident my flair for atmosphere and characterization would sparkle alongside the numbing mulch ground out by studio hacks. Certainly the space atop my mantel might be better festooned by a gold statuette than by the plastic dipping bird that now bobbed there ad infinitum. The notion of taking a brief hiatus from my serious writing to amass a nest egg that could subsidize my *War and Peace* or *Madame Bovary* was not an unreasonable one to contend with.

And so, clad in author's tweeds with elbow patches and Connemara cap, I ascended to the Royal Suite of the Carlyle Hotel to rendezvous with the self-proclaimed titan E. Coli Biggs.

Biggs was a fubsy pudding of a character with a hairpiece that could only have been ordered by dialing 1-800-Toupees. A farrago of tics animated his face in unpredictable dots and dashes like Morse code. Clad in pajamas and the Carlyle's terrycloth robe, he was accompanied by a miraculously fabricated blonde who doubled as secretary and masseuse, having apparently perfected some foolproof procedure to clear his chronically stuffed sinuses.

"I'll come right to the point, Mealworm," he said nodding toward the bedroom, where his zaftig protégée rose and weaved off to, pausing a mere two minutes to align the meridians of her garter belt.

"I know," I said, descending from Venusburg. "You read

my book, you're taken with how visual my prose is, and you'd like me to create a scenario. Of course you realize even if we got copacetic on the math, I would have to insist on total artistic control."

"Sure, sure," Biggs mumbled, waving aside my ultimatum. "You know what a novelization is?" he asked, popping a Tums.

"Not really," I replied.

"It's when a movie does good numbers. The producer hires some zombie to make a book out of it. Y'know, an exploitation paperback—strictly for lowbrows. You've seen the chozzerai you find in the racks at airports or shopping malls."

"Uh-huh," I said, beginning to sense a lethal tightness making its deceptively benign introduction into my lumbar region.

"But me, I'm to the manor born. I don't hondle with mere craftsmen. I meld exclusively with bona fides. Hence I'm here to report your latest tome caught my baby blues last week at a little country store. Actually I'd never seen a book remaindered in the kindling section before. Not that I got through it, but the three pages I managed before narcolepsy set in told me I was in the presence of one of the most egregious wordsmiths since Papa Hemingway."

"To tell you the truth," I said, "I've never heard of novelizations. My métier is serious literature. Joyce, Kafka, Proust. As for my first book, I'll have you know the cultural editor of *The Barber's Journal*—"

"Sure, sure, meanwhile every Shakespeare's gotta eat lest he croak ere he mints his magnum opus."

"Uh-huh," I said. "I wonder if I might have just a little water. I've become rather dependent on these Xanax."

"Believe me, kid," Biggs said, raising his voice and intoning slowly. "All the Nobel laureates work for me. It's how they set their table." Poised in the wings, his stacked amanuensis pushed her head in and trilled, "E. Coli, García Márquez is on the phone. Claims his larder is bereft of all provender. Wants to know if you can possibly throw any more novelizations his way."

"Tell Gabo I'll get back to him, cupcake," snapped the producer.

"And just what movie are you asking me to novelize?" I piped, gagging on the word. "Are we talking about a love story? Gangsters? Or is it action-adventure? I'm known as a facile man with description, particularly bucolic material à la Turgenev."

"Tell me about the Russkies," Biggs yelped. "I tried to make Stavrogin's confession into a musical for Broadway last year, but all the backers suddenly got swine flu. Here's the scam, tatellah. I happen to own the rights to a cinema classic starring the Three Stooges. Won it years ago playing tonk with Ray Stark at Cannes. It's a real zany vehicle for our three most irrepressible meshoogs. I've fressed all the protein I can out of the print—movie houses, foreign and domestic TV— but I suspicion there's still a little lagniappe to be bled from a novel."

"Of the Three Stooges?" I asked, incredulous, my voice glissandoing directly into a fife's octave.

"I don't have to ask if you love 'em. They're only an institution," Biggs pitched.

"When I was eight," I said, rising from my chair and slapping at my pockets to locate my emergency Fiorinal.

"Hold it, hold it. You didn't hear the plot yet. It's all about spending the night in a haunted house."

"It's OK," I said, dollying toward the door. "I'm a little late—some friends are raising a barn—"

"I booked a projection room so I could screen it for you," Biggs said, ignoring my resistance, which by now had morphed into sheer panic.

"No thanks. I may be down to my last can of StarKist," I sputtered as the great man cut me off.

"Emmes, kid. If this is as lucrative as my proboscis signals, there's copious zuzim to be stockpiled. Those three ditsy vilda chayas cut a million shorts. One e-mail could secure the novelization rights to the whole shooting match. And you'd be my main scribe. You could salt away enough mad money in six months to spend the rest of your days sausaging out art. Just give me a few sample pages to confirm my faith in your brilliance. Who knows, maybe in your hands novelization will finally come of age as an art form."

That night I clashed fiercely with my self-image and required the emollient waters of the Cutty Sark distillery to beat back a waxing depression. Still, I would be disingenuous if I did not admit that I was palpated by the notion of vacuuming up enough scratch to allow the writing of another masterpiece without the onset of malnutrition. But it was not just Mammon crooning in my cochlea. There was also the chance Biggs's nasal compass had located true north. Perhaps I was the Mahdi chosen to legitimize with depth and dignity this runt of the literary litter, the novelization.

In a frenzy of sudden euphoria I bolted to my processor, and irrigated with gallons of black coffee, I had by dawn broken the back of the challenging assignment and was champing at the bit to show it to my new benefactor.

Irritatingly, his Do Not Disturb did not come unglued till noon, when I finally rang through as he was masticating his morning fiber.

"Be here at three," he bade. "And ask for Murray Zangwill. Word leaked of my quondam alias, and the joint's awash with frenzied centerfolds panting for screen tests." Pitying the man's beleaguered existence, I spent the next hours honing several sentences to diamond perfection and at three entered his posh digs with my work retyped on a stylish vellum.

"Read it to me," he commanded, biting off the tip of a contraband Cuban cigar and spitting it in the direction of the fake Utrillo.

"Read it to you?" I asked, taken aback over the prospect of presenting my writing orally. "Wouldn't you rather read it yourself? That way the subtle verbal rhythms can resonate in your mind's ear."

"Naw, I'll get a better feel this way. Plus I lost my reading glasses last night at Hooters. Commence," ordered Biggs, putting his feet up on the coffee table.

"Oakvill, Kansas, lies on a particularly desolate stretch

across the vast central plains," I began. "What's left of the area where farms once dotted the landscape is arid space now. At one time corn and wheat provided thriving livelihoods before agricultural subsidies had the opposite effect of enhancing prosperity."

Biggs's eyes began to glaze over. His head was wreathed in a thick nimbus of smoke from the vile cheroot.

"The dilapidated Ford pulled up before a deserted farmhouse," I went on, "and three men emerged. Calmly and for no apparent reason the dark-haired man took the nose of the bald man in his right hand and slowly twisted it in a long, counterclockwise circle. A horrible grinding sound broke the silence of the Great Plains. 'We suffer,' the dark-haired man said. 'O woe to the random violence of human existence.'

"Meanwhile Larry, the third man, had wandered into the house and had somehow managed to get his head caught inside an earthenware jar. Everything was suddenly terrifying and black as Larry groped blindly around the room. He wondered if there was a god or any purpose at all to life or any design behind the universe when suddenly the dark-haired man entered and, finding a large polo mallet, began to break the jar off his companion's head. With pent-up fury that masked years of angst over the empty absurdity of man's fate, the one named Moe smashed the crockery. 'We are at least free to choose,' wept Curly, the bald one. 'Condemned to death but free to choose.' And with that Moe poked his two fingers into Curly's eyes. 'Oooh, oooh, oooh,' Curly wailed, 'the cosmos is so devoid of any justice.' He stuck an unpeeled banana in Moe's mouth and shoved it all the way in."

At this point Biggs abruptly emerged from his stupor. "Stop, go no further," he said, standing at attention. "This is only magnificent. It's Johnny Steinbeck, it's Capote, it's Sartre. I smell money, I see honors. It's the kind of quality product yours truly made his rep on. Go home and pack. You'll stay with me in Bel Air till more suitable quarters open up— something with a pool and perhaps a three-hole golf course. Or maybe Hef can put you up at the mansion for a while if you'd prefer. Meantime I'll call my lawyer and lock up rights to the entire Stooge oeuvre. This is a memorable day in the annals of Gutenbergsville."

Needless to say, that was the last I saw of E. Coli Biggs under that or any other alias. When I returned to the Carlyle, valise in hand, he had long left town for either the Italian Riviera or the Turkmenistan Film Festival or possibly to check out the bottom line in Guinea-Bissau—the desk clerk wasn't sure. The point is, tracking down a mover and shaker who never uses his real name proved a far too daunting job for an ink-stained wretch named Mealworm, and I'm dead certain it would have been for Faulkner or Fitzgerald too.

Calisthenics, Poison Ivy, Final Cut

‍

As a hatchling chloroformed and shanghaied each summer to various lakeside facilities bearing Indian names where I struggled to master the dog paddle under the baleful eyes of capos otherwise known as counselors, my attention was pinioned recently by something in the back pages of *The New York Times Magazine*. Amongst the usual dumping grounds where well-heeled parents might stash their sniveling issue and savor a comatose July and August were ads for such trendy modern specialties as basketball camp, magic camp, computer camp, jazz camp, and, perhaps the most glamorous of all, film camp.

Apparently somewhere amidst the crickets and ragweed a teenager with a yen for montage can idle away his sunny vacation learning to churn out Oscar-winning dialogue, proper camera angles, acting, editing, sound mixing, and, for all I know, the correct way to buy a home in Bel Air complete with valet parking. While less dream-weaving adolescents are busy foraging for arrowheads, a number of budding Von Stroheims actually get to make their own original movies, a far hipper summer project than, say, braiding a lanyard to dangle one's skate key from.

This pricey inspiration seems a long way from Camp Melanoma, run by Moe and Elsie Varnishke in Loch Sheldrake, where I suffered the dog days of my fourteenth year playing dodgeball and keeping the calamine-lotion industry solvent. It was not easy to picture a mom-and-pop couple like the Varnishkes running anything resembling so chic a venue as film camp, and only the fumes of a smoked whitefish I was deconstructing at the Carnegie Deli induced sufficient hallucinatory molecules to conjure the following correspondence.

Dear Mr. Varnishke:

Now that fall has descended, gifting the foliage with her sublime palette of rust and amber, I must pause in the day's occupation here on Wall and William to thank you for providing my cherished offspring Algae with a rich and productive summer at your traditional yet innovative rustic paradise. His tales of hiking and canoeing startle in their similarity to passages by Sir Edmund Hillary and Thor Heyerdahl. They add just the proper curry to the diligent and intense hours he spent with you acquiring the various techniques of filmmaking. That his eight-week movie turned out so accomplished and exciting that Miramax is offering us sixteen million dollars for the domestic rights is more than any parent could have dreamed of, although it was always clear to his mother and I that Algae was anointed by the muses.

What did surprise me for just a nanosecond, however, was the letter you wrote suggesting that 50 percent of the afore-mentioned distribution fee should somehow find its way into your pocket. How a sweet couple like you and Mrs. Var-nishke could cobble together the psychotic mirage that you are somehow entitled to the faintest taste of my son's creative fruits beggars all rationality. In short, let me assure you that despite the fact that his cinematic masterpiece took wing at the ramshackle little Hooverville represented in your brochure as Hollywood in the Catskills, you have absolutely zero tithe to any portion of my flesh and blood's windfall. I guess what I am trying to find a nice way of saying is, you and that avaricious salamander that shares your bed whom I hap-pen to know put you up to this mail-fisted shakedown should take a flying hike.

Cordially,
Winston Snell

Mine Dear Mr. Snell:

Thanking you so much for the prompt reply to mine note and the beautiful admission that your son's motion picture owes its whole everything to our charming country resort de-scribed in what I guarantee will soon become Exhibit A as a Hooverville. Speaking, by the way, of Elsie, there never was a finer woman despite some smoker-car witticisms you passed when you came to visit, highlighting her varicose veins, which drew no laughs even from the busboys, who hate her like rat poison. You should know before you open up a mouth with the salamander jokes that my wife is a dedicated woman who suffers from a curse called Ménières, and believe me when I tell you she can't get out of bed in the morning without she ricochets off the chifforobe. You should have such a malady—I'm sure you wouldn't play tennis so fast every week at the Athletic Club with your cronies with the plaid pants, all waiting to be indicted. I personally don't make six figures speculating with other people's pensions. I run a nice honest film camp, which my wife and I started from pennies we saved from the candy-store days when maybe if we sold a few extra pairs of wax lips we could afford carp once a week.

Meanwhile your son's film was made under the supervision or, better I should say, collaboration of our crackerjack staff, which, take it from Varnishke, any of the big studios should only have, they wouldn't grind out such chozzerai always for ten-year-old submentals. A man like Sy Popkin who personally spitballed concepts with the little nudnik happens to be one of Hollywood's great unrecognized talents. The man could have won fifty Academy Awards if he hadn't one lousy time been spotted in Mexico double-dating with Trotsky, a coincidence that forever marked him unhirable with those schmendriks who right away run scared. Also our dramatics counselor, Hydra Waxman, who gave up a promising screen career to donate, gratis yet, her time to teaching teenage golems. The woman—may she rest in peace but later, after she dies—personally directed the amateur cast in your son's movie, coaxing from a tsimmes of talentless trombeniks every tiny morsel of histrionic ability while meanwhile your little momser sat on the sidelines watching her work and breathing from his adenoids.

Finally, Mr. Wall Street macher, there's our own Abe Silver-fish, a man who has editing awards from prestige film festivals in Tanganyika and Bali. The man stood—and if I'm lying my wife should perish in an acid bath—stood over and badgered your schlimazel Algae, who if you take my advice you'd toss the kid a little Ritalin once in a while maybe he would now and then stop with the fidgeting. Silverfish personally stood over the Avid and showed him where he should make every splice. Incidentally, the kid used all our equipment, fiddling like the klutz he is with a brand-new Panavision camera, which now when I press the button makes a sound like when you turn slowly the wood handle on those tin party noisemakers Elsie calls groggers. Meanwhile for this I wouldn't bill you since we're about to be partners in a new venture.

Respectfully,
Monroe B. Varnishke

Dear Mr. Varnishke:

To suggest in any way that the staff you have assembled is anything higher on the evolutionary scale than a band of dingoes is hyperbole of the wildest sort. Partners in a new venture?! Have you suffered a silent stroke? First let me be clear that the idea for Algae's screenplay was conceived by my son alone and based on true life experience that the family lived through when our local mortician mistakenly thought he'd won the Nobel Prize. That a traitor like Popkin who probably passed atomic secrets to Trotsky over tacos might have in any way contributed as much as a comma to my wunderkind's scenario ranks in credibility alongside accounts of the Loch Ness monster. As for that dipso Miss Hydra Waxman, the Internet tells me that she has never appeared in any film of a millimeter above eight, and then under the name of Candy Barr. Incidentally, are you aware your instructor Silverfish was fired from editing a Hollywood movie because Henry Fonda was repeatedly cut in upside down? Algae also said the camera you provided him with, far from being new, ran in fits and starts as a result of being heaved at a nineteen-year-old lifeguard when she refused your advances. Is Mrs. Varnishke OK with you hitting on the female help? By the way, I apologize for disparaging your wife's circulatory system with my sometimes too accurate wit. Given the myriad blue tributaries that mark her topography, I couldn't keep myself from commenting on her similarity to a road map.

Finally, let this be the termination of any contact between us. All further correspondence should be mailed directly to the firm of Upchuck and Upchuck, Attorneys-at-Law.

Au revoir, meatball.

Winston Snell

Mine Dear Mr. Snell:

I only thank God He gave me a sense of humor so I can take a little joshing without immediately running right away to one of those gun magazines where hit men are so easy to hire. Let me do you a favor and clear up for you some facts. I never once in forty years looked at another woman except for Elsie, which candidly was not so easy as I'm the first to admit she's not a dish like those zaftig courvers who pose in God knows what positions for magazines you probably wait drooling on the docks for as the boats arrive from Copenhagen.

Secondly, I'm just curious—where did you get the idea that that little vontz your son was a wunderkind? It could only be that you're a typical cigar-sucking money maven who surrounds himself with namby-pambies who yes you and fill you full of bubbe meisehs you like to hear and the minute you leave the room, believe me, they roll their eyes. When Elsie and I had the candy store and I had a cretin who jerked my sodas who I kept on out of the goodness of my heart for his mother, she had a hip replacement, the doctors made a mistake, she wound up with a Chinaman's liver—anyhow, this poor troll, the soda maker, with his double-digit IQ, towered like Isaac Newton over your Algae mentally.

That, by the way, was the summer Elsie's nephew Benno won the spelling bee. "Mnemonic" the kid spelled, he's all of eight. This is what I call bright, not your blond Midwich cuckoo who's had every advantage in every private school with the expensive tutors and still he can't remember who he is without checking the name tape in his T-shirt.

Meanwhile, instead of threatening with the lawsuits, tell instead your shysters if they check carefully, they'll see that while you have a single print of the film that made both Weinstein brothers run like a couple of land speculators to throw sixteen million rugs your way, we have the only existing original negative up here in a bungalow. I just pray nothing happens to it, not that Mrs. Varnishke hasn't already gotten a chicken-fat stain on the opening shot.

Moe Varnishke

Varnishke:

I read your last letter with a mixture of pity and fear, the Aristotelian recipe for tragedy. Pity because you obviously are unaware that by holding the negative to my son's film you are guilty of a little social lapse called grand larceny, and fear because I had a prophetic dream last night wherein, after your prison sentence, you vividly caught a screwdriver in the tripes from a burly fellow inmate at Angola.

Although a fresh negative can be minted, albeit one of inferior quality, from the print I have, I would strongly suggest you instantly ship the original to yours truly before further defiling of its delicate coating occurs from either chicken fat or any other of the assorted noisome condiments you and that gargoyle that stares back at you over the breakfast table uses to render edible her cuisine. My patience is rapidly expiring.

Winston Snell

Listen, Snell:

It's you not me that's heading to the slammer and if not for trying to sell a movie you don't own by yourself then for at least kiting checks because your genius son talks in his sleep and Elsie's hobby is taping. Meanwhile I try to protect the negative but believe me it's not easy. First my nephew Shlomo, he's six next week, such a lovely kid, can sing all the words to "Ragmop" in either Yiddish or English. But let's face it, it's a wild age and he took a sharp rock and put a long scratch right in the middle of reel two. He loves to take the negative out of the can and scrape the emulsion off with a penknife. Why? Do I know? I just know he scrapes and he kvells. Not to mention my sister Rose got Lubriderm on reel seven. The poor woman. Her husband died recently, a massive heart attack, but I warned him—don't look directly at her when she steps out of the shower. Anyhow, it's a shame you're so stubborn because by now we both could be realizing a nice piece of change from this flick, but listen, you're a man with principles. By the way, exactly what is kiting checks, and why is it a felony? Gotta go, the dog has the negative.

Varnishke

Varnishke:

You vile little paramecium. I offer you a 10 percent participation in the distribution rights to Algae's film. What you really deserve, in your own vernacular, is not one red cent but a good spritz from a can of Raid.

I suggest you grab this deal before I regain my balance and take it off the table as it could be your passport from the grubby summer world of pubescent auteurs to the delights of Miami or Bermuda. Perhaps if some portion of your profits goes to a good plastic surgeon for a complete physical makeover, Mrs. Varnishke might even be allowed on a public beach.

Winston Snell

Mine dear boy:

Elsie regained consciousness from a coma she was in, the result of an accident she had setting some mousetraps, she leaned in too far to smell the cheese to make sure it was fresh. Bingo! Anyhow, she woke up just long enough to whisper into my ear the words "Make it twenty percent." Then, out again like one of those dolls when you tilt it back the eyes close. Meanwhile, the minute you put on the dotted line your Sam Hancock—and before a notary she also mentioned— you'll not only get the negative but Elsie makes a wonderful stuffed cabbage which we'll include gratis a few portions but return the jars please. You should live and be well.

Your new partner,
Moe Varnishke

NANNY DEAREST

❧

"WHAT EVIL LURKS in the hearts of men? The Shadow knows." And with that came a fiendish cackle projecting shivers up my spine every Sunday when as a mesmerized youth I sat curled around our Stromberg Carlsen in the crepuscular winter light of my progenitors' gloomy digs. The truth is, I never had the slightest idea what dark mischief gadded about even in my own pair of ventricles, until weeks back when I received a phone call from the better half at my office at Burke and Hare on Wall Street. The woman's usual steady timbre jiggled like quantum particles, and I could tell she had gone back on smokes.

"Harvey, we must talk," she announced, her words fairly drenched in portent.

"Are the children all right?" I snapped, expecting at any moment to be read the text of a ransom note.

"Yes, yes, but our nanny—our nanny—that smiling and unfailingly polite Judas, Miss Velveeta Belknap."

"What about her? Don't tell me the twit's gone and broken another Toby mug."

"She's writing a book about us," the voice on the other end intoned as though emanating from a catacomb.

"About us?"

"About her experiences being our Park Avenue nanny for the past year."

"How do you know?" I rasped, suddenly crippled by remorse that I had pooh-poohed legal counsel advising a confidentiality agreement.

"I went to her room while she was out to return two Tic Tacs I had borrowed before the holidays, when I inadvertently came across a manuscript. Naturally I couldn't resist a peek. Darling, it's vicious and embarrassing beyond anything you can imagine. Especially the parts about you."

A twitching in my cheek began its arrhythmic calisthenics, and drops of perspiration began emerging on my brow with audible snaps.

"As soon as she gets home I'm going to fire her," the Immortal Beloved said. "The snake refers to me as porcine."

"No! Don't fire her. That won't stop the book and will only cause her to dip her quill in more astringent vitriol."

"What then, lover boy? You know how these revelations will play amongst our tony chums? We won't be able to set foot at any of the posh watering holes we habituate without we're snickered at and lampooned by wit's cruel rapier. Velveeta refers to you as 'that gnarled little pipsqueak who buys his hapless offspring into top preschools while failing to do yeoman service in the boudoir.' "

"Don't do anything till I get home," I pleaded. "This requires a little skull session."

"You better ratiocinate on the double, sugar. She's up to page three hundred." With that, the light of my life smashed the phone down into its cradle with photon velocity, causing my ears to ring with the ominous tolling of that damn bell in Donne's poem. Feigning Whipple's disease, I bailed out of my work early, pausing at the corner hops emporium to placate my jangled ganglia and review the crisis.

Our history with nannies had been a roller-coaster ride at best. The first one was a Swedish woman who resembled Stanley Ketchel. Her demeanor was succinct, and she achieved discipline amongst the brood, who began showing up for meals well mannered but with inexplicable contusions. When our hidden TV camera caught her in the act of bouncing my son horizontally across her shoulders in what wrestlers call the Argentine backbreaker, I queried the woman on her methods.

Obviously unused to interference, she lifted me out of my loafers and pinioned me to the wallpaper a good three feet off the floor. "Keep your schnozz out of my rice bowl," she advised, "unless you're happy to wind up in a reef knot."

Outraged, I sent her packing that night, requiring the assistance of only a single SWAT team.

Her successor, a nineteen-year-old French au pair named Veronique, who was all wiggles and cooing, with blond hair, the pout of a porn star, long tapered legs, and a rack that almost required scaffolding, was a far less truculent type.

Her commitment to our issue, unfortunately, lacked a certain depth, preferring as she did to loll about on the chaise in a slip and vaporize chocolate truffles while thumbing the pages of *W*. I adjusted to the creature's personal style more flexibly than my wife did and even attempted to help her relax with an occasional back rub, but when the ball and chain noticed I had taken to wearing Max Factor and bringing the little frog breakfast in bed she tucked a pink slip into the folds of Veronique's *poitrine* and deposited her Louis Vuitton on the curb.

And then came Velveeta, a pleasant drone pushing thirty who ministered to the children and knew her place at table. Moved by her strabismus, I had treated Velveeta more like a family member than a servant, yet all the while as she accepted second helpings of trifle and access on her off-hours to the comfy chair, she was secretly amassing an unflattering portrait of her benefactors.

Upon arriving home and perusing in secret her libelous narrative, I was rendered dumb.

"A bitter cipher who takes credit for his colleagues' work at the firm," the succubus had written. "A raving bipolar who at once spoils his children and then beats them with a razor strop for the slightest infractions." I leafed through the vile compilation and was mortified by the smorgasbord of blasphemies.

> Harvey Bidnick is a witless boor, a motormouthed little proton who fancies himself amusing but numbs his guests

with relentless one-liners unfunny even on the borscht circuit fifty years ago. His imitation of Satchmo causes the bravest souls to flee screaming from the room. Bidnick's wife is no bargain either. A portly ice queen with tapioca thighs, she is unable to process any references intellectually more complex than Manolo Blahnik and Prada. The couple fight incessantly, and on one occasion when she had run up a bill of six figures for a specially constructed Wonder Bra, Bidnick refused to pay it. Enraged, she snatched the toupee from his head, threw it to the floor, and fired several shots at it with a revolver they keep in case of burglars. Bidnick gorges himself on Viagra, but the dosage makes him hallucinate and causes him to imagine he is Pliny the Elder. His wife, aging like Maria plucked from Shangri-La, has had every inch of her body tweaked with either Botox or a scalpel. Their favorite topic of conversation is the denigration of friends. The Birdwings are "corpulent penny-pinchers who serve small portions with the mutton inevitably underdone." Dr. Diverticulinsky and his wife are a "team of incompetent veterinarians who have been responsible for the death of more than one goldfish." And the Offals are "that French couple whose depravities include sexual intimacies with the figures at Madame Tussaud's."

I put down the pages of Velveeta's tell-all screed, went to our bar, knocked back a series of potently configured highballs, and resolved then and there to kill her.

"If we burn her pages, she'll just run off a duplicate," I prattled to my wife in speech starting to loosen like a vaudeville drunk's. "If we offer her hush money, she'll include the bribe in her memoir or pocket the jack and publish anyway. No, no," I said, morphing into all the blackguards that populated the noir celluloid I grew up on. "She must be made to disappear. Naturally it should look like an accident. Perhaps a hit-and-run."

"You don't drive, blue eyes," the steely minx opposite me clarified, draining her own personal beaker of gin and vermouth. "And our chauffeur, Measly, couldn't hit the side of a barn with that triple-length white stretch Lincoln you make him tool around in."

"Well, what about a bomb?" I fonfered. "A precision device carefully timed to go off just as she boards her Stair-Master."

"Are you kidding?" the light of my life croaked, succumbing a bit more to her grain concoction. "You couldn't make a bomb if they handed you the plutonium. Remember Chinese New Year's when you dropped that lit Roman candle down your trousers?" The little woman started laughing hoarsely. "Christ, the way you suddenly rose off the ground and passed over the garage roof in Quogue. What a trajectory!" she howled.

"Then I'll push her out the window. We'll forge a note or, better yet, dupe her into writing one herself under some clever pretext utilizing carbon paper."

"You're going to hoist a hundred-fifty-pound nanny up to the windowsill and force her out while she struggles? With your biceps? You'll wind up in Lenox Hill Emergency with a myocardial infarction that'll make Krakatoa seem like a hiccup."

"You don't think I can dispose of her?" I said, marinating rapidly from my fifth grasshopper and dissolving into an Alfred Hitchcock character. "She will be free to move about, but she will be on a chain. She will gradually grow more and more ill." I visualized the out-of-focus camera that made the audience at *Notorious* feel Ingrid Bergman's weakening point of view as Claude Rains's poison took its toll. My own focus had gone a little soft too as I rose and teetered to the medicine cabinet, my fingers closing around the bottle of iodine. As if on cue, the door burst open and Velveeta entered.

"Hey, Mr. B, you're home. Get fired? Ha ha." The rodent smiled at her own insolent sally.

"Come in," I said. "Just in time for coffee."

"You know I don't drink coffee," she demurred.

"I meant tea," I corrected, staggering to the kitchen to put on the kettle.

"Are you plastered again, Mr. B?" the judgmental wretch inquired.

"Sit here," I directed, ignoring her churlish familiarity. By now my wife had collapsed and was snoring on the floor.

"Mrs. B's got to get more sleep," the smug babysitter chided as she winked. "What do you jaded plutocrats do all night?" With a mastermind's cunning I glanced over my shoulder to see that she was not looking and emptied the remains of the iodine bottle into Velveeta's cup. Then, festooning a plate with succulent petit fours, I presented the arrangement to her.

"Gee," she piped, "this is something new. We never tore a herring at eleven-thirty in the A.M."

"Hurry," I said, "let's drink up before it gets cold."

"Isn't this a little dark for chamomile?" the perfidious fink whined.

"Nonsense," I explained. "It's a rare blend, just in from Lashkar Gāh. Come, drink up. Umm, how smoky and piquant."

Perhaps it was the stress of the morning, perhaps it was the concatenation of confidence builders I downed before noon; all I know is somehow I managed to siphon the mickeyed teacup by mistake. Instantly I jackknifed and began to flap around on the floor like a snagged trout. I lay on the carpet clutching my stomach and moaning like Ethel Waters singing "Stormy Weather" while our alarmed nanny commandeered an ambulance.

I remember the faces of the paramedics, and the stomach pump, and I remember most clearly, when I came to fully, the notice Velveeta handed in. She said in her letter of resignation that she had become bored being a nanny, and had toyed with writing a book but chucked the idea because the lead characters were too creepy to hold the interest of any reader with an

IQ in the normal range. She was leaving to marry a million-aire who picked her up one day at the Alice statue where she often took our kids. As for the Bidnicks? We don't plan to hire another nanny until there's a huge technological break-through in robotics.

How Deadly Your Taste Buds, My Sweet

‿❧

The snob value of the rare white truffle hit new heights in London on Sunday with a 2.6-pound specimen selling at auction for $110,000. It went to an unidentified buyer in Hong Kong.

—*The New York Times,* November 15, 2005

As a private eye I'm willing to take a bullet for my clients, but it'll cost you five hundred Benjamins per hour plus expenses, which usually means all the Johnnie Walker I can knock back. Still, when a cupcake like April Fleshpot totes her pheromones into my office and requests servicing, the work can magically become pro bono.

"I need your help," she purred, crossing her legs on the sofa while her black silk hose took no prisoners.

"I'm all ears," I said, confident that the sexual irony in my inflection wasn't wasted.

"I need you to go to Sotheby's and bid on something for me. Naturally I'll foot the bill. But it's important I remain anonymous." For the first time I was able to see beyond her blond hair, pillow lips, and the twin dirigibles that stretched her silk blouse to the breaking point. The kid was scared.

"What do I bid on?" I asked her, "and why can't you do it?"

"A truffle," she said, lighting a cigarette. "You can go as high as ten million dollars. Well, maybe twelve if the competition is keen."

"Uh-huh," I said, throwing her the glance I usually flash before dialing Bellevue. "You must have a real craving."

"Oh, don't be crass," she snapped back, clearly miffed. "You'll get double your usual fee. Just don't leave Sotheby's without it."

"Suppose I said anything over five million dollars seems a little suspicious for a mushroom," I needled her.

"Maybe—although the Bundini truffle went for twenty million, the highest price on record for a tuber at auction. Of course it had been owned by the Aga Khan and was flawless white. And don't fail me, because I was outbid recently on some foie gras by a Texas oilman who topped my seven million with eight. This was after I had sold two Chagalls to raise the cash."

"I remember seeing that foie gras in the Christie's catalogue. Seemed like big bucks for an appetizer-sized portion. But, if it made the oilman happy."

"He was murdered for it," she said.

"No."

"Yes. A count from Romania, for whom nothing but the taste of sublime goose liver would suffice, slipped a dirk between his shoulder blades and pirated the moist patty," she said, lighting another cigarette from her first.

"Hard luck," I said, staring at her.

"The joke was on him, though," she laughed. "The high-cholesterol treat he had killed for turned out to be a fake. You see, the count, in a gesture of love, laid the foie gras at the feet of the grand duchess of Estonia, and when she unmasked it as liverwurst, he took his own life."

"And the real foie gras?" I inquired.

"It was never recovered. Some say it had been noshed by a Hollywood producer at Cannes. Others said an Egyptian named Abu Hamid was so taken with it he packed it in a syringe and tried shooting it directly into his veins. Still others said it had fallen into the hands of a housewife from Flatbush who thought it was cat food and fed it to her tabby."

April opened her pocketbook, pulled out a check, and wrote my retainer.

"Just one thing," I said. "Why can't anyone know you want the truffle?"

"A network of gourmands originating in Istanbul and frantic to shave it over their fettucini has infiltrated our borders. They will stop at nothing to obtain the truffle. Any single woman possessing such a taste treat puts her life in grave jeopardy."

Suddenly I got a cold chill. The only prior case I'd ever had involving a pricey edible was a relatively simple business concerning a portobello mushroom. There had been charges of inappropriate behavior toward it by a political aspirant, but the allegations proved baseless. The deal was, I bring the truffle to Suite 1600 of the Waldorf, where, April said flirtatiously, she'd await me in something skin-colored that God had designed for her. Once she wiggled her award-winning posterior into the lift, I made a few transatlantic phone calls to Fortnum & Mason's and Fauchon. Their managers owed me for a little favor I did them once, by recovering six priceless anchovies purloined by a dacoit. When I got the skinny on April Fleshpot, I cabbed over to York Avenue.

The bidding at Sotheby's was spirited. A quiche went for three million, a matched pair of hard-boiled eggs fetched four, and a shepherd's pie once belonging to the Duke of Windsor sold for six million. When the truffle came on the block, a buzz shot through the room. Bidding started at five million dollars, and once the weak sisters faded I found myself in a tennis match with a fat man who wore a fez. At twelve million smackers the porky plutocrat had enough and dropped out, visibly distraught. I claimed the 2.6-pound dingus, stashed it in a locker at Grand Central, and made a beeline for April's suite.

"Did you bring the truffle?" she asked, opening the door in a satin robe with nothing but well-dispersed protoplasm under it.

"Don't worry," I said, flashing a tough smile. "But first, shouldn't we talk numbers?" The last thing I remember before the lights went out was a collision between the top of my head and what felt like a shipment of bricks. I awoke to the glint of a Saturday night special aimed directly at that little valentine-shaped pump I use to facilitate my blood flow. The fat man in the fez from Sotheby's was tickling the safety catch for my amusement. April sat on the sofa, her pretty cheekbones buried in a Cuba Libre.

"Well, sir, let's get down to business," the fat man said, laying a baked potato on the table.

"What business?" I smirked.

"Come now, sir," he wheezed. "Surely you understand we're not discussing an ordinary ascomycetous mass. You have the Mandalay truffle. I want it."

"Never heard of the thing," I said. "Oh, wait—wasn't that playboy Harold Vanescu beaten to death with it in his Park Avenue apartment last year?"

"Ha ha, you amuse me, sir. Let me tell you the history of the Mandalay truffle. The emperor of Mandalay was married to one of the fattest, homeliest women in the land. When swine flu claimed all the pigs in Mandalay, he asked his wife if she would be willing to root out the truffles. The moment she sniffed it, its value was instantly clear to all and it was sold to the French government and put on exhibition at the Louvre. It remained there and was looted by German soldiers during World War II. It's said Göring was seconds away from eating it when news of Hitler's suicide put a damper on the meal. After the war the truffle vanished and turned up on the international black market, where a consortium of businessmen purchased it and brought it to DeBeers in Amsterdam in an attempt to have it cut and then sell the pieces individually."

"It's in a locker at Grand Central," I said. "Kill me and the best you'll ever decorate that spud with will be sour cream and chives."

"Name your price," he said. April had gone into the other room and I heard her place a call to Tangiers. I thought I heard the word "crêpes"—apparently she had raised the money for the first payment on a major crêpe but en route to Lisbon the filling had been switched.

Fifteen minutes after I named my price, my secretary brought over a package weighing 2.6 pounds and placed it on the table. The fat man unwrapped it with trembling hands and, with his penknife, sliced off a slim piece to sample. Suddenly he began hacking at the truffle in a wild rage and sobbing.

"My God, sir!" he screamed. "It's a fake! And while it's a brilliant fake, counterfeited to simulate some of the truffle's nutlike flavor, I'm afraid what we have here is a large matzo ball." In an instant he was out the door, leaving me alone with a stunned goddess. Shaking off her dismay, April lasered her aqua orbs into mine.

"I'm glad he's gone," she said. "Now it's just you and I. We'll track down the truffle and split it. I wouldn't be surprised if it held aphrodisiac powers." She let her robe slip open just enough. I came very close to surrendering to all the absurd gymnastics nature programs the blood for, but my survival instinct kicked in.

"Sorry, sweetheart," I said, backing off. "I don't intend to wind up like your last husband, at the city fridge with a tag on my toe."

"What?" Her face went ashen.

"That's right, toots. It was you who killed Harold Vanescu, the international gourmet. It didn't take a quiz kid to dope it out." She tried to bolt. I blocked the door.

"OK," she said resignedly. "I guess my number's up. Yes, I killed Vanescu. We met in Paris. I had ordered caviar at a restaurant and had cut myself on one of the toast points. He came to my aid. I was impressed with his haughty disdain for red eggs. At first things were wonderful. He showered me with gifts: white asparagus from Cartier's, a bottle of expensive balsamic he knew I loved to dab behind my ears when we went out. It was Vanescu and I who stole the Mandalay truffle from the British Museum by hanging upside down from ropes and cutting through the glass case with a diamond. I wanted to make a truffle omelet, but Vanescu had other ideas. He wanted to fence it and use the money to buy a villa in Capri. At first nothing had been too good for me; then I noticed the portions of beluga on our crackers were getting smaller and smaller. I asked him if he was having trouble in the stock market, but he pooh-poohed the idea. Soon I realized he had secretly switched from beluga to sevruga, and when I accused him of using osetra in a blini, he became irritable and noncommunicative. Somewhere along the line he had turned budget-conscious and frugal. One night I came home unexpectedly and caught him preparing hors d'oeuvres with lungfish caviar. It led to a violent quarrel. I said I wanted a divorce, and we argued over custody of the truffle. In a moment of rage I picked it up from the mantel and struck him with it. When he fell, he hit his head on an after-dinner mint. To hide the murder weapon I opened the window and threw it onto the back of a passing truck. I've been searching for it ever since. With Vanescu out of the way, I truly believed I could finally scarf it up. Now we can find it and share it—you and I."

I remember her body against mine and a kiss that caused steam to jet out of both my ears. I also remember the look on her face when I turned her in to the NYPD. I sighed over her state-of-the-art equipment as she was cuffed and led away by the fuzz. Then I beat it over to the Carnegie Deli for a pastrami on rye with pickles and mustard—the stuff that dreams are made of.

Glory Hallelujah, Sold!

❧

The Internet auction site eBay has gained a new spiritual dimension, with a seller offering prayers for cash. The self-styled Prayer Guy, based in Co. Kildare, Ireland, is selling five prayers, with bidding for each of them starting at £1. Buyers with pressing spiritual needs can buy immediately for £5.

—Item in church newsletter, August 2005

WHEN THE RATINGS came out and *The Dancing Ombudsman* got a minus thirty-four, there was some talk at Nielsen that people who accidentally tuned in the show then put their eyes out like Oedipus. In the end the bottom line prevailed and our staff was assembled in the office of the producer, Harvey Nectar, and each writer was offered a choice between resignation or going into a closed room with a revolver. I won't downplay my responsibility as a participant in what *Variety* called "a fiasco comparable to the meteor that wiped out the dinosaurs," but I will say in my defense that I was basically a punch-up specialist put in at the last minute to leaven the burn-unit scenes with sight gags.

The last few seasons working on the tube have been a little rough on me, and it seems the many flop series my name has appeared on proceeded one after the other with the relentless consistency of carpet bombing. My agent, Gnat Louis, was taking longer and longer to return my phone calls, and finally, when I collared him over salmon cheeks at Nobu, he leveled with me and pointed out that to the industry the credit Hamish Specter on an end crawl was a synonym for potassium cyanide.

Unbent by the turn of events yet requiring a minimal ration of caloric material in order to remain amongst the living, I scoured the want ads and happened to come across a curious one in *The Village Voice*. The proposition read: "Bard wanted to write special material—good pay—no atheists please."

Skeptic that I was as an adolescent, I had recently come to believe in a Supreme Being after thumbing through a Victoria's Secret catalogue. Figuring this might be the yellow-brick to a little fresh scratch, I shaved and donned my most solemn attire, a black three-button number that would have been the envy of any pallbearer. Computing the tariff for private transportation versus the subway, I made a beeline for the IRT and jiggled to Brooklyn, where, above Rocky Fox's Stick Academy, a green felt parlor with the usual cast of unsavories nursing their cue balls, existed the national headquarters of Moe, the Prayer Jockey.

Far from ecclesiastical in feel, the offices I entered bustled with the whirligig energy of *The Washington Post*. There were cubbies all over where harried scribes were banging out prayers to meet what was obviously an enormous demand.

"Come in," a corpulent presence beckoned as he laid waste a covey of rugelach. "Moe Bottomfeeder, the Prayer Jockey. What can I do you for?"

"I saw your ad," I wheezed. "In the *Voice*. Right under the Vassar coeds who specialize in body rubs."

"Right, right," Bottomfeeder said, licking his fingers. "So, you want to be a psalm scrivener."

"Psalms?" I queried. "Like 'The Lord is my shepherd'?"

"Don't knock it," Bottomfeeder said, "it's a big seller. You should be so lucky. Any experience?"

"I did do a TV pilot called *Nun for Me, Thanks,* about some very devout sisters in a convent who build a neutron bomb."

"Prayers are different," Bottomfeeder said, waving me off. "They gotta be reverent, plus they gotta give hope, but—and here's what separates the truly gifted minter of supplications from your Hallmark hacks—the prayers have gotta be worded in suchwise that when they don't come true, the mark—er, that is, the faithful—can't sue. You follow me?"

"I think I do. You'd prefer to avoid costly litigation," I bantered.

Bottomfeeder winked. His bespoke threads and Rolex suggested a crackerjack business mind not unlike Samuel Insull or the late Willie Sutton.

"Believe it or not, I began as a lower-class drone like yourself," he said, launching unasked into his formative years. "Starting out selling neckties from an open valise à la Ralph Lauren. Both of us hit it big. Him in fashion, me by skinning the flock. Let's face it, most people have pressing spiritual needs. I mean, every cretin prays. Using the old dreidel, I knocked out a couple of plaintive invocations on my laptop and the ginch I was bouncing at the time got the lightbulb to auction them off on eBay. Pretty soon the demand got so great I had to put on a staff. We got prayers for health, for love problems, for that raise you want, the new Maserati, maybe a little rain if you're a rube—and of course the ponies, the point spread, and our hottest item: 'O Heavenly Father, Lord God of hosts, let me abide in the kingdom of glory forever and, just once, hit the lottery—oh, and Lord, the Megaball.' Like I say, the wording's gotta be such that should the heavenly request tank, we don't wind up getting served."

At this point the door clicked open and a troubled head popped in. "Hey, boss," the confounded author yelped, "a guy in Akron wants a prayer so his wife should bear him a son. I'm stymied for a fresh approach."

"Oh, I forgot to tell you," Bottomfeeder said to me, "I recently added a service where we customize prayers. We fashion the text to the unworthy's individual needs and mail him some personally tailored begging." Then, turning to his minion, he barked, "Try 'May the broad lie down in green pastures and drop foals abundantly.'"

"Brilliant, M.B.," the writer said. "I knew if I was stuck for a sacred phrase—"

"No, wait," I interjected suddenly. "Make that 'May she multiply fruitfully.' "

"Hey," Bottomfeeder said, "you're cooking with gas. This kid's a pheen." I was basking in my compliment when the phone rang. Bottomfeeder pounced on it.

"Holy Moe Bottomfeeder, the Prayer Jockey, speaking. What? I'm sorry, lady. You have to talk to our complaint department. We do not guarantee the Lord will grant whatever it is you're on about. He can only give it His best shot. But don't get discouraged, sweetheart. You still may find your cat. No, we don't give refunds. Read the tiny letters on your prayer-confirmation contract. Spells out our liability and His. What we will do, though, is send you one of our complimentary blessings, and if you go over to the Lobster Grotto on Queens Boulevard and tell 'em the Lord sent you, you'll get a gratis cocktail." Bottomfeeder hung up. "Everybody's on my case. Last week I got sued because we mailed the wrong envelope to a woman. She wanted a little divine assistance to make her face work turn out swell, and I accidentally sent her a prayer for peace in the Middle East. Meanwhile Sharon pulls out of Gaza and she gets off the operating table looking like Jake LaMotta. So what do you say, chuckles, in or out?"

Integrity is a relative concept, best left to the penetrating minds of Jean-Paul Sartre or Hannah Arendt. The reality is, when winter winds howl and the only affordable dwelling shapes up as a cardboard carton on Second Avenue, principles and lofty ideals have a tendency to vanish in a whirlpool down the bathroom plumbing, and so, postponing plans for a

Nobel, I gritted my teeth and leased my muse to Moe Bottom-feeder. For the following six months, I must confess, a myriad of those pleas for divine intervention you or yours may have requested or bid for on eBay were knocked out by Mrs. Specter's onetime prodigy, Hamish. Among my gold-leaf texts were "Dearest Lord—I am only thirty and already balding. Restoreth mine hair and anoint my sparse areas with frankincense and myrrh." Another Specter classic: "Lord God, King of Israel—I have tried but in vain to shed twenty pounds. Smite my excess avoirdupois and protect me from starches and carbs. Yea, as I walk through the valley, deliver me from cellulite and harmful trans fats."

Perhaps the top price ever paid at a prayer auction was for my moving plea: "Rejoice, O Israel, for the stock market hath arisen. O Lord, can You do it now for the Nasdaq?"

Yes, the Benjamin Franklins were falling into my account like manna from heaven until one day two swarthy gentlemen, heavily invested in Sicilian cement, dropped up to the office while Bottomfeeder was out. I was at my desk, debating the ethics of a prayer for some new home owners pleading for the castration of their contractor. Before I could ask the visitors how I could help them, I found myself making the same sound a fife makes as the one named Cheech lifted me by the scruff of my neck and dangled me out the window, high above Atlantic Avenue.

"There must be some mistake," I squealed, scrutinizing the pavement below with more than a vested interest.

"Our sister won a prayer here last week," he said. "She bid high on eBay for it."

"Yes—yes," I gagged. "Mr. Bottomfeeder will be back at six. He handles—"

"Well, we're here to give you a message. That co-op board better accept her," Cheech explained.

"We hear you wrote that prayer," the brother with the ice pick added. "Let's hear it—and loud."

Not wanting to deny their request and seem a spoilsport, I trilled the material in question in the manner of Joan Sutherland.

"Blessed art Thou, oh Lord. Grant me in thine infinite wisdom the two-bedroom with the eat-in kitchen on Park and Seventy-second."

"She paid twelve hundred bucks for that prayer. It better come true," Cheech said, snapping me back inside and hanging me on the coatrack like a duck in a Chinatown window.

"Either that or we mail your arms and legs to four different addresses." With that they quit the offices of Moe Bottomfeeder, Prayer Jockey, and after making sure they were long gone, so did I.

I don't know if the building in question finally accepted Teresa Calebrezzi as a tenant, but I can say that while there are not many writing jobs here in Tierra del Fuego, my kneecaps are still of a piece. Amen.

CAUTION, FALLING MOGULS

⚬✑

WHILE PERUSING THE *Times* movie ads in desperate search of some bearable celluloid high jinks with which to palliate a summer of heat and barometric readings one associates with August in Yoknapatawpha County, I had the interesting fortune to find a little oddment entitled *The Kid Stays in the Picture.* This nostalgic documentary chronicled the rise of a young Prince Charming from a minor acting role as a matador to a taurine Hollywood studio head, laid low by the banderillas of blind ambition, marital heartbreak, and the untimely foreclosure by public servants of a commodious stash of nose candy. Emotionally shredded by this Euripidean tragedy, I eschewed sleep that night to mint a screenplay on the theme of hubris in Lotusland—a manuscript that promises to be an artistic and commercial event unexperienced since *Howard the Duck.* Some scenes follow.

Fade in on a papaya stand on Manhattan's West Side. Dispensing franks and coconut milk is a hangdog pilgrim in his fifties whose prematurely aging visage speaks eloquently of

*suffering at fate's mercurial whims. He is Mike Umlaut,
who muses to himself ruefully while drawing a piña colada
as his boss, Mr. Ectopic, looks on.*

UMLAUT   Saints preserve me. That I, Mike Umlaut, once re-
splendent CEO of a dream factory, vacuuming profits like a
slot machine, am reduced to doling out tropical beverages
as a means of keeping my stove warm.

ECTOPIC   Let's move it, Umlaut. There's a customer bellowing for a corn dog.

UMLAUT   Right away, sir. Just slicing a papaya in such wise
as to retain its healthful vitamin content. (*To himself, as he
fetches a corn dog for an insistent eight-year-old*) Ironic
that I who began my career trafficking in victuals should
end up in similar fashion.

(*Camera shakes as we dissolve back to Umlaut's first job as
caterer on the set of* Where Beavers Fear to Tread, *a studio
epic shot at a lot close to Paramount. We dolly in to the
craft-service table, where we discover Harry Eppis, the producer, pondering the assorted pick-me-ups.*)

EPPIS (*to Moribund, his yes-man*)   What to do? Here I am,
two years over schedule on an eight-week shoot, and my
lead actor, Roy Reflux, gets busted for frottage at the Gap.
Is it a wonder my ulcer's the size of a flapjack? You there,
wretched caterer: black coffee and a cinnamon Danish.

MORIBUND   You'll have to shoot around him, H.E. At least
till his parole. It'll add copious zeroes to our budget, but
you knew Reflux was a handful when you inked his pact.

UMLAUT   Excuse me, sir, for daring to speak, but I couldn't
help overhearing your little dumka. Why not just write his
role out?

EPPIS   What? Who said that? Do my cochleas deceive me, or
was it the lowly purveyor of buns?

UMLAUT   Think of it, sir. His character, though amusing, is
not pivotal. A few lashes laid to the writer's back and he
could emend the scenario with sufficient cunning as to
manumit you forever from Reflux, that pot of kasha, whom
you're vastly overpaying, if *Variety*'s any judge.

EPPIS   I'll bet he's right. This below-the-line inchworm has just
brushed a veil from before my peepers. You've a quick nog-
gin, you rascal—and obviously it extends beyond schnecken.

UMLAUT   By the way, I wouldn't have black coffee and cinnamon Danish if you have an ulcer. The one is sodden with
caffeine, the other sports too savory a spice. Why not let me
coddle you a more user-friendly tandem of *oeufs*.

EPPIS   Is there no end to this Renaissance man's vision?
There's a place for a noodle such as yours in the front office. Henceforth you will be in charge of all pictures made
at Bubonic Studios.

(*Dissolve to a movie premiere at Grauman's Chinese The-atre. The words "One Year Later" are supered over the glittering throng that engorges the lobby. An admixture of moguls and superstars exchange insincerities with agents, directors, and ravishing young wannabes. The camera trav-els down the chandelier, à la Hitchcock, to a close-up of Mike Umlaut's trembling hands as he converses, sotto voce, with his newly acquired agent, Jasper Nutmeat.*)

NUTMEAT   Take it easy, kid. I've never seen you so wired.

UMLAUT   Wouldn't you be, Nutmeat? My first picture as producer. If *Behold a Pale Endocrinologist* doesn't make it, I'm finished. Fifty million simoleons suctioned from studio coffers and deposited in perpetuity with Thomas Crapper.

NUTMEAT   You gotta go with your instinct, kid. Your gut told you America's ready for a picture about the smelting process.

UMLAUT   I've only staked my future on it. But what am I to do, Nutmeat? I'm a dreamer.

(*A velvety voice punctuates Umlaut's reverie.*)

PAULA   And I'd like a chance to make your dreams come true.

(*Umlaut snaps around and we cut to a blond apparition in her early twenties, clearly descended from Olympus by way of Hugh Hefner's mansion.*)

UMLAUT Wha? Who are you, you fortuitous agglomeration of protoplasm?

PAULA Paula Pessary. I'm only a starlet now, but with a teensy break I could lay siege to the hearts of a truly solid demographic.

UMLAUT And I'll see to it you get the at-bat so coveted.

PAULA (*stroking his cheek*) I promise you, I'm well trained in the art of gratitude.

(*The bow tie of Umlaut's tuxedo begins spinning like a propeller.*)

UMLAUT I mean to marry you and make you the brightest star in the firmament, and I'm including Canis Major, the dog one.

PAULA Mike Umlaut marry? Everyone knows that as Tinseltown's budding Thalberg you're glimpsed nightly at sundry boîtes always squiring a fresh mouse.

UMLAUT Till tonight. Tonight, the earth shook.

NUTMEAT (*running over*) The reviews are in. The movie's a smash. You'll never have to return another phone call!

(*Cut to exterior shot of Bubonic Studios. Cut inside to reveal the new head honcho, Mike Umlaut. He sits in his office, where the walls are dotted with Warhols and Stellas, plus an occasional Fra Angelico to limn the breadth of his taste. Surrounding him are flunkies and myrmidons aplenty. Nutmeat, now a vice president, is present, plus Arvide Mite and Tobias Gelding, two ubiquitous studio dealmakers. Dolly in for two-shot of Umlaut barking orders to his harried secretary, Miss Onus.)*

UMLAUT Get me Wolfram Ficus on the phone and tell him I'm sending him a copy of *Such Foolish Chickens*. Tell him to read the part of Yount the apothecary. And ready my private Gulfstream; there's a sneak preview of *The Reluctant Embalmer* in Seattle. Have the plane taxi down Rodeo Drive and pick me up in front of Spago after lunch.

GELDING M.U., the weekend figures are in. *Gerbils and Gypsies* has broken every record at the music hall.

MITE As has *The Learning Disabled Toreador*. Everything you touch goes platinum.

UMLAUT Say, boys, have any of you read *Gilgamesh*?

(They assent enthusiastically.)

NUTMEAT The Babylonian Bible? Sure, several times, why?

UMLAUT I'm going to say one word to you: musical.

NUTMEAT (*reverentially*) Only you. Only you . . .

(Paula Pessary, now Mrs. Umlaut, enters in a tight Versace dress that breads her voluptuous contours like matzo meal on a cutlet.)

PAULA   The advance notices of *Reverse Peristalsis* are in. They're calling me this generation's Garbo and you the brooding Svengali who pulls the strings.

(*Umlaut produces a tiara from his pocket and lays it on her. They kiss.*)

GELDING   Isn't love something? Clock this golden couple. While flood and famine cloak so much of the blue marble, these two coast through, buttressed only by devotion and high grosses.

(*Dissolve to the set of a film on location in Coonabarabran. The director, Lippo Sheigitz, is raging at Umlaut.*)

SHEIGITZ   You crass philistine! This was supposed to be my picture! I was to have total artistic control!

UMLAUT   What's a few line changes?

SHEIGITZ   Line changes? The blind concert violinist is now a Navy SEAL?

UMLAUT   It gives more oomph. Look, Sheigitz, you know that I'm not one of those passive suits who just busy themselves with arithmetic. I'm a creative, hands-on guy. By the way, forget Mozart, I've decided it's going to be a rock score. I've hired the group Epicac to handle the music.

SHEIGITZ (*attacking Umlaut with a prop hoe*)   I'll dismember you, you ham-fisted meddler!

(*Guards rush in and remove Sheigitz.*)

NUTMEAT Not to worry, M.U. He'll be replaced *toot sweet* by a more malleable weaver of dreams. Town's full of 'em. Say, why the ductile puss? Don't let that ersatz auteur put you uptight.

UMLAUT It's not that. It's Paula, my wife.

NUTMEAT Uh-oh, what gives, M.U.?

UMLAUT She's been having an affair with her co-star, Agamemnon Wurst. And who can blame her? Workaholic that I am, I turned a blind eye when she went off to make a film on location in Paris with the number one box-office attraction in America. The film wrapped two years ago, and they're still on location. It doesn't take much to put the pieces together.

NUTMEAT That gonzo? You could ruin him in the business with one phone call.

UMLAUT No, I prefer the high road. I wished them Godspeed. Funny, we once vowed eternal love—now she won't tell me where she hid the car keys.

(*Cut to chopper landing, and an excited Arvide Mite runs at Umlaut.*)

MITE What figures—what gorgeous numerals. The remake of *Love Tsimmes* is a monster hit. M.U., you could film the L.A. phone directory and make it into a bonanza.

NUTMEAT   You've got a wild look in your eyes, M.U. I've never discerned it before. Add a crooked Jekyll-and-Hyde smile. I pray you're not about to overreach.

(*Musical sting. Dissolve to six months later. Umlaut's Holmby Hills estate. Here, as in his office, the walls are littered with Rauschenbergs and Johnses, with a casual sprinkling of Vermeers to leaven the modernity. Nutmeat is consoling Umlaut as a half dozen impassive furniture movers are removing paintings and repossessing everything he owns.*)

NUTMEAT   Did I say take it easy? Did I not lecture myself blue in the punim on overweening ambition, using as a for instance Icarus?

UMLAUT   Yes, but—

NUTMEAT   What but? Arvide Mite was only waxing hyperbolic when he said you could make the phone book into a hit. Only an idiot or a megalomaniac would have accepted the challenge. Especially the Yellow Pages.

UMLAUT   What did I do?

NUTMEAT   What you've done is taken a record budget of two hundred million iron men and fabricated a concrete latke that opened to bupkis. I guess you can't blame the board of directors of Amalgamated Sushi for ousting you. That Japanese conglomerate's going to have to sell a lot of yellowtail to break even.

(*As the last of Umlaut's furniture is toted off, he is picked up bodily by local marshals and heaved into the service alley while a family of Bedouins drop anchor on the property. We dissolve back to the present, to find Umlaut scurrying to fill an order of Orange Nectars for six impatient hard hats. A car pulls up to the curb, and Umlaut's lawyer, Nestor Weakfish, emerges, waving a document.*)

WEAKFISH   Umlaut! Umlaut, your faithful Solon bears news.

UMLAUT   If it's about the retainer, I'm tapped.

WEAKFISH   Stop blathering. All is roses. Our claim against Amalgamated Sushi took years, but we've won it.

UMLAUT   You mean, the studio's no longer contesting my golden-parachute clause?

WEAKFISH   You got it. Under your deal, the termination of your contract sluices them to the tune of six hundred million clams. My boy, you've been made whole!

UMLAUT (*tearing off his apron*)   I'm rich! Six hundred million! I can buy this whole papaya chain and fire Mr. Ectopic. I can buy my house back, my airplane, my Vermeers!

WEAKFISH   Hey, wait a minute—we beat a sushi conglomerate. I said six hundred million clams—we're talking bivalves here.

(Weakfish gestures outside as a refrigerated truck starts unloading Umlaut's settlement. As Umlaut turns on Weakfish with a shucking knife, the camera pulls back and rises on a crane to view it all from on high, paying homage to the shot of the wounded Confederacy in Gone with the Wind, *while we fade to black.)*

THE REJECTION

WHEN BORIS IVANOVICH opened the letter and read its contents he and his wife, Anna, turned pale. It was a rejection of their three-year-old son, Mischa, by the very best nursery school in Manhattan.

"This can't be," Boris Ivanovich said, stricken.

"No, no—there must be some mistake," his wife concurred. "After all, he's a bright boy, pleasant and outgoing, with good verbal skills and facile with crayons and Mr. Potato Head."

Boris Ivanovich had tuned out and was lost in his own reveries. How could he face his co-workers at Bear Stearns when little Mischa had failed to get into a preschool of reputation? He could hear Siminov's mocking voice: "You don't understand these matters. Connections are important. Money must change hands. You're such a bumpkin, Boris Ivanovich."

"No, no—it isn't that," Boris Ivanovich heard himself protest. "I greased everybody, from the teachers to the window washers, and still the kid couldn't hack it."

"Did he do well at his interview?" Siminov would ask.

"Yes," Boris would reply, "although he had some difficulty stacking blocks—"

"Tentative with blocks," Siminov whined in his contemptuous fashion. "That speaks for serious emotional difficulties. Who'd want an oaf that can't make a castle?"

But why should I even discuss all that with Siminov? Boris Ivanovich thought. Perhaps he won't have heard about it.

The following Monday, however, when Boris Ivanovich went into his office it was clear that everyone knew. There was a dead hare lying on his desk. Siminov came in, his face like a thundercloud. "You understand," Siminov said, "the lad will never be accepted at any decent college. Certainly not in the Ivy League."

"Just because of this, Dmitri Siminov? Nursery school will impact on his higher education?"

"I don't like to mention names," Siminov said, "but many years ago a renowned investment banker failed to get his son into a kindergarten of ample distinction. Apparently there was some scandal about the boy's ability to finger paint. At any rate, the lad, having been rejected by the school of his parents' choice, was forced to . . . to . . ."

"What? Tell me, Dmitri Siminov."

"Let's just say that when he turned five he was forced to attend . . . a public school."

"Then there is no God," Boris Ivanovich said.

"At eighteen his onetime companions all entered Yale or

Stanford," Siminov continued, "but this poor wretch, never having acquired the proper credentials at a preschool of—shall I say—appropriate status, was accepted only at barber college."

"Forced to trim whiskers," Boris Ivanovich cried, picturing poor Mischa in a white uniform, shaving the wealthy.

"Having no substantial background in such matters as decorating cupcakes or the sandbox, the boy was totally unprepared for the cruelties life held," Siminov went on. "In the end, he worked at some menial jobs, finally pilfering from his employer to keep up an alcohol habit. By then he was a hopeless drunkard. Of course, pilfering led to thievery and ended up with the slaughter of his landlady and her dismemberment. At the hanging, the boy attributed it all to failing to get into the correct nursery school."

• • • •

THAT NIGHT, Boris Ivanovich could not sleep. He envisioned the unattainable Upper East Side preschool, with its cheerful, bright classrooms. He pictured three-year-olds in Bonpoint outfits cutting and pasting and then having some comforting snack—a cup of juice and perhaps a Goldfish or a chocolate graham. If Mischa could be denied this, there was no meaning in life or in all of existence. He imagined his son, a man now, standing before the CEO of a prestigious firm, who was quizzing Mischa on his knowledge of animals and shapes, things he would be expected to have a deep understanding of.

"Why . . . er," Mischa said, trembling, "that's a triangle—no, no, an octagon. And that's a bunny—I'm sorry, a kangaroo."

"And the words to 'Do You Know the Muffin Man?' " the CEO demanded. "All the vice presidents here at Smith Barney can sing them."

"To be honest, sir, I never learned the song properly," the young man admitted, while his job application fluttered into the wastebasket.

IN THE DAYS following the rejection, Anna Ivanovich became listless. She quarreled with the nanny and accused her of brushing Mischa's teeth sideways rather than up and down. She stopped eating regularly and wept to her shrink. "I must have transgressed against God's will to bring this on," she wailed. "I must have sinned beyond measure—too many shoes from Prada." She imagined that the Hampton Jitney tried to run her over, and when Armani canceled her charge account for no apparent reason, she took to her bedroom and began having an affair. This was hard to conceal from Boris Ivanovich, since he shared the same bedroom and asked repeatedly who the man next to them was.

When all seemed blackest, a lawyer friend, Shamsky, called Boris Ivanovich and said there was a ray of hope. He suggested they meet at Le Cirque for lunch. Boris Ivanovich arrived in disguise, since the restaurant had refused him admittance when the nursery-school decision came out.

"There is a man, a certain Fyodorovich," Shamsky said, spooning up his portion of crème brûlée. "He can secure a second interview for your offspring and in return all you have to do is keep him secretly informed of any confidential information about certain companies that might cause their stocks to suddenly rise or fall dramatically."

"But that's insider trading," Boris Ivanovich said.

"Only if you're a stickler for federal law," Shamsky pointed out. "My God, we're talking about admission to an exclusive nursery school. Of course, a donation will help as well. Nothing showy. I know they're looking for someone to pick up the tab for a new annex."

At that moment, one of the waiters recognized Boris Ivanovich behind his false nose and his wig. The staff fell upon him in a fury and dragged him out the door. "So!" the headwaiter said. "Thought you'd fool us. Out! Oh, and as for your son's future, we're always looking for busboys. Au revoir, beanbag."

At home that night, Boris Ivanovich told his wife they would have to sell their home in Amagansett to raise money for a bribe.

"What? Our dear country house?" Anna cried. "My sisters and I grew up in that house. We had an easement that cut through a neighbor's property to the sea. The easement ran right across the neighbor's kitchen table. I remember walking with my family through bowls of Cheerios to go swimming and play in the ocean."

As fate would have it, on the morning of Mischa's second

interview his guppy passed away suddenly. There had been no warning—no previous illness. In fact, the guppy had just had a complete physical and was pronounced in A1 health. Naturally, the boy was disconsolate. At his interview he would not touch the Lego or the Lite Brite. When the teacher asked him how old he was, he said sharply, "Who wants to know, lard bucket?" He was passed over once again.

Boris Ivanovich and Anna, now destitute, went to live in a shelter for the homeless. There they met many other families whose children had been turned down by elite schools. They sometimes shared food with these people and traded nostalgic stories of private planes and winters at Mar-A-Lago. Boris Ivanovich discovered souls even less fortunate than himself, simple folk who had been turned down by co-op boards for not having sufficient net worth. These people all had a great religious beauty behind their suffering faces.

"I now believe in something," he told his wife one day. "I believe there is meaning in life and that all people, rich and poor, will eventually dwell in the City of God, because Manhattan is definitely getting unlivable."

Sing, You Sacher Tortes

∼

Not since the evanescence of Hubert, whose flea museum enchanted the naïfs on Forty-second Street, has the Broadway area seen a shyster to rival that peerless purveyor of schlock Fabian Wunch. Balding, cheroot-sucking, and as phlegmatic as the Wall of China, Wunch is a producer of the old school, resembling physically not so much David Belasco as "Kid Twist" Reles. Given the consistency and dimensions of his exaltation of flops, it has remained a puzzle on a par with string theory how he manages to raise money for each fresh theatrical holocaust.

Hence, when a beefy arm in a Sy Syms suit curled itself around my shoulder blades the other day as I perused some Rusty Warren at the Colony record shop, and the heady conflation of lilac Pinaud and stale White Owls subverted my hypothalamus, I could feel the wallet in my pocket instinctively clenching like an endangered abalone.

"Well, well," a familiar raspy voice said, "just the man I want to see."

I was among the legally insane who had put money in several of Wunch's sure things over the years, the last being *The Henbane Affair,* a West End import that chronicled the invention and manufacture of the adjustable showerhead.

"Fabian!" I squealed with affected congeniality. "We haven't spoken since your rather nasty brouhaha with the opening-night critics. I've often wondered if spraying them with Mace didn't actually make matters worse."

"I can't talk here," the simian impresario said furtively, "lest some nudnik get wind of a concept that is positively guaranteed to transmogrify our net worths to a number only astronomers could make sense of. I know a little bistro on the Upper East Side. Buy me lunch and I may be able to bless you with partnership in a diversion the mere road companies of which will keep your children's children in rubies the size of breadfruit."

Were I a squid, this preamble alone would have been more than enough to trigger the ejaculation of black ink, and yet before I could scream for the riot police I found myself sucked up and flip-screened crosstown to a modest French restaurant, where, for as little as two hundred and fifty dollars per person, one could eat like Ivan Denisovich.

"I've analyzed all the great musicals," Wunch said to me as he ordered a '51 Mouton and the tasting menu. "And what do they have in common? Let's see if you know."

"Great music and lyrics," I ventured.

"Well, naturally, boob. That's the easy part. I got an undiscovered genius mints hit songs like the Japs roll off Toyotas. Right now the kid walks dogs for a living, but I've been privy to his oeuvre, and it's everything Irving Berlin would have liked to have been if things had broken differently for him. No, the key is a great book. That's where I come in."

"I never knew you to put pen to paper," I said as Wunch vacuumed a concatenation of escargots from their shells.

"So our show," he continued. "*Fun de Siècle*—and *notez bien* the mischievous wordplay in the title, on account of it transpires totally in Vienna."

"Contemporary Vienna?" I asked.

"No, dum-dum—a hoarier epoch, with all the broads in carriages and gowns à la *My Fair* or *Gigi*. Not to mention the myriad freaky bohemians who wax Looney Tunes all over the Ringstrasse. Only Klimt, only Schiele, only Stefan Zweig, plus a pretty fair country doodler who answers to Oskar Kokoschka."

"Illustrious figures all," I chimed in, as Wunch's cheeks flushed crimson in homage to the Bordeaux region of France.

"And which fox do all these name brands go ape over?" he went on. "The love interest? A local sex bomb named Alma Mahler. You must've heard of her. She bounced 'em all—Mahler, Gropius, Werfel. You name 'em, they rifled her thong."

"Well, I don't know—"

"Well, I know. I mean, sure, I'm taking subtle license with the narrative. Otherwise, kid, we midwife a soporific. I'm modernizing the language too. Like when Bruno Walter runs into Wilhelm Furtwängler and says, 'Hey, Furtwängler, will you be at Rilke's barbecue Saturday night?' And Furtwängler says, 'Barbecue?,' like it's clear he wasn't invited, and Walter says, 'Oops, sorry—I guess I shouldn't have opened my big yap.' See, the talk's got a today urban rhythm."

As Wunch bore down on his hot foie gras, I could feel the onset of a growing numbness in several of my key vertebrae, and I loosened my tie in an effort to breathe.

"So," he waxed on, "first comes the overture, which I see as light and catchy but in the twelve-tone scale—as a nod to Schoenberg."

"But, surely, with all those lovely Strauss waltzes—" I cut in.

"Don't be an Ignatz," Wunch said with a dismissive wave. "Those we save for the finale, when the audience is panting for relief from two hours of atonality."

"Yes, but—"

"Then the curtain goes up and the sets are in the style of the Bauhaus."

"The Bauhaus?"

"Like form follows function. In fact, the opening song is Walter Gropius, Mies van der Rohe, and Adolf Loos singing 'Form Follows Function,' like 'Fugue for Tinhorns' begins *Guys and Dolls*. It finishes and who enters but Alma Mahler herself, in a frock Jennifer Lopez would wave off as skimpy. With Alma is her composer husband, Gustav. 'Let's go, gloom puss,' she says. 'Move it.'

" 'Just one more strudel,' the fragile tunesmith replies. 'I need the blood-sugar high to keep me from sinking into my quotidian preoccupation with mortality.'

"Meanwhile, while this is going on," Wunch elaborated, "Gropius is giving Alma the eye, which she's turned on by, and she sings, 'I'd Love to Be Groped by Gropius.' Scene One ends with a blackout and when Scene Two lights up, she's living with Gropius and cheating on him with Kokoschka."

"What happened to her husband, Gustav?" I queried.

"What do you think? He's eyeballing the Danube, nursing a big jones for Alma, and ready to do a Brodie when who bicycles by but Alban Berg."

"No!"

" 'What obtains, Mahler? Not looking to take the coward's way out, are you?' he inquires. Mahler lays his marital meshugas on him, and Berg tells him he's got just the thing. Berg says there's this bearded cat, lives at 19 Berggasse, and for a few pfennig an hour—which for some reason the guru has emended to fifty minutes, don't ask me why—he can get his sconce tightened."

"Nineteen Berggasse? Wait a minute, Mahler was never a patient of Freud's," I protested.

"It's OK. I made him a compulsive stutterer, which piques Freud. A childhood trauma. Mahler once witnessed a local burgomaster drown in Schlag. Now he relives it. A couch is lowered, center stage, and Freud sings a great comedy number, 'Just Say the First Thing That Comes to Mind.' Naturally, being Freud, it's all double entendre and we take the mickey out of Viennese mores, showing that even a great writer of symphonies like Mahler is subconsciously hung up on corsets, beer, and ragtime, albeit he sets his table mining the sublime. Freud unblocks Mahler so he can write again, and as a result Mahler triumphs over his lifelong fear of death."

"How does Mahler triumph over his fear of death?" I asked.

"By dying. I figured it out—it's really the only way."

"Fabian, there are a few holes here. You didn't give Mahler a writer's block. You said he was despondent over losing Alma."

"Exactly," Wunch said. "That's why he sues Freud for malpractice."

"But if he's dead, how can he sue?"

"I didn't say the story didn't need a polish, but that's what Boston and Philly are for. OK, so at this point Alma is shacking up with Kokoschka, but now she's diddling Gropius. You get the irony? She sings 'Cozy with Kokoschka,' but a minor chord in the verse tells the audience different. Plus I wrote this killer scene when Gropius accuses Kokoschka in a café of defacing his recently completed office building. 'So, Kokoschka,' he says, 'it's you which slathered an opaque ichor on my latest architectural breakthrough, the new Chozzerai Towers.' Whereupon Kokoschka goes, 'If you call those dull boxes of yours architecture, then, yes, it was me.' Enraged, Gropius hurls his portion of Tafelspitz at Kokoschka, momentarily blinding him, and demands satisfaction."

"Wait a minute," I said. "Those two great giants never fought a duel."

"Nor do they in our little cash cow, because at the last second Werfel arrives, disguised as a chimney sweep, and Alma goes off with him, leaving the pair of heartbroken swains to sing what may be the most biting piece of sophistication in Broadway history: 'My Pretty Little Schnitzel, You're the Wurst.' End of Act One."

"I don't get it. Why would Werfel be disguised as a chimney sweep? And I still say if Mahler is dead, how will he and Alma get back together the way they actually did in life?"

I was full of probing questions; much better to ask them now before a less tolerant paying audience elected instead to pass out disemboweling equipment.

"Werfel had to conceal his identity," Wunch explained, "because Kafka's in town and wants back an only copy of his new short-story masterpiece, which he lent Werfel, and which Werfel, short of confetti for a parade, was forced to dice. As far as Alma and Gustav's rapprochement goes, in Act Two she cheats on Werfel with Klimt and then betrays Klimt by posing nude for Schiele."

"But—"

"Don't tell me it never happened. All those broads in garter belts Schiele drew—why couldn't one be of Alma Mahler? But it doesn't matter, because before you can say 'Franz Josef' she cops a sneak on Schiele and Klimt, and as we come to the middle of Act Two she's cohabiting with none other than his nibs Mr. Ludwig Wittgenstein. The two duet on 'Of Things We Cannot Speak We Must Remain Silent.' But it doesn't work out, because when Alma says 'I love you' to Wittgenstein, he parses the sentence and disproves the definition of each word. The chorus dances the birth of linguistic philosophy, and Alma, hurt, yet with her libido intact, belts out 'Pet Me, Popper.' Enter Karl Popper."

"Hold it!" I said, with visions of an audience fleeing up the aisles en masse like migrating caribou. "You never explained to me, since when have you turned author? I always knew you to be happy with a producer's credit."

"It's since the accident," Wunch replied, meticulously spooning up the last few molecules of profiterole. "The beloved and I were hanging a picture when she tried driving a nail into the wall and inadvertently coldcocked me with a ball-peen hammer. I must've been on queer street a good ten minutes. When I awoke, I found I could write every bit as well as Chekhov or Pinter. This whole shmegegge I just walked you through was created during a single shave. Hey, isn't that Stevie Sondheim just came in? Count to fifty, I'll be back. Want to lay a notion on him before he vanishes on me again. Poor guy must be aging. Last time he gave me his phone number, one digit was off. Settle up and I'll detail the finale for you over a Courvoisier."

And with that he table-hopped his way over to a man who resembled the author of *A Little Night Music*. The last image I had as I pricked my finger and signed the check in O-negative was of Wunch lowering himself uninvited into a booth amid the cacophonous objurgations of its abashed occupant. As far as me backing *Fun de Siècle*, there's an old theater superstition that any show in which Franz Kafka sprinkles sand on the stage and does a soft-shoe is just too big a risk.

ON A BAD DAY YOU CAN SEE FOREVER

~❧~

MEMBERS OF one fairly tony New York health club
dove for cover this summer as the rumbling sound
that usually precedes a fault separation reverberated through
their morning workout. Fears of an earthquake were soon al-
layed, however, as it was discovered that the only separation
was a shoulder of mine, which I had mangled trying to tickle
pink the almond-eyed fox who did push-ups on the adjoining
mat. Eager to catch her eye, I had attempted to clean and jerk
a barbell equal in weight to two Steinways when my spine
suddenly assumed the shape of a Möbius strip, and the lion's
share of my cartilage parted audibly. Emitting the identical
sound a man makes when he is thrown from the top of the
Chrysler Building, I was carried out in a crouch and rendered
housebound for all of July. Utilizing the enforced bed rest, I
turned for solace to the great books, a mandatory list I had
been meaning to get to for the past forty years or so. Arbi-
trarily eschewing Thucydides, the Karamazov boys, the dia-
logues of Plato, and the madeleines of Proust, I hunkered
down with a paperback of Dante's *Divine Comedy,* hoping to

revel in tableaux of raven-tressed sinners looking like they'd come directly from the pages of a Victoria's Secret catalogue as they undulated, seminude, in sulfur and chains. Unfortunately, the author, a stickler for the big questions, quickly dislodged me from that gauzy dream of erotica, and I found myself gadding about the nether regions with no steamier a persona than Virgil to broadcast the local color. Somewhat of a poet myself, I marveled at how Dante had brilliantly structured this subterranean universe of just deserts for life's mischief makers, rounding up various poltroons and miscreants, and doling to each his appropriate level of eternal agony. It was only when I finished the book that I noticed he had left out any special mention of contractors, and with a psyche still vibrating like a sock cymbal from having renovated a house some years prior, I could not but wax nostalgic.

It all began with the purchase of a small brownstone on Manhattan's Upper West Side. Miss Wilpong, of Mengele Realtors, promised us it was the buy of a lifetime, priced modestly at a figure no higher than the cost of a stealth bomber. The dwelling was drumbeat as being in "move-in condition," and perhaps it was, for the Jukes family or a caravan of Gypsies.

"It's a challenge," my wife said, breaking the women's indoor record for understatement. "This will be so fun to redo." Sidestepping some loose floorboards, I tried to remain upbeat and likened its charm to that of Carfax Abbey.

"Picture we lose this wall and make a big California kitchen," the distaff ranted. "There's space for a study, and each child can have her own room. With a little plumbing work we can have separate bathrooms, and I bet you could even have that game room you always wanted—to leaven your more philosophical moments with some pinball."

While fantasies of the beloved's architectural megalomania raced unchecked, the wallet in my breast pocket began to flutter like a hooked flounder. Visions of squandering all I'd carefully husbanded over years of labor while punching up eulogies for the Schneerson Brothers Burial Home caused me to take issue in the upper register of the piccolo. "You really think we need this place?" I said, praying the urge to own would abate like a petit mal.

"What I love about it is that it has no elevator," the Better Half cooed. "Can't you just picture what going up and down those five flights will do for your ticker?"

Short of embezzlement, the means to pay for this new venture were beyond me, and it took a song-and-dance man's personality to secure a mortgage from skeptical bankers, who at first waved me off but softened when they found a loophole in the usury laws. Selecting an appropriate contractor came next, and as the bids drifted in I couldn't help noticing that most of the prices quoted seemed more appropriate for a renovation of the Taj Mahal. In the end I settled on a suspiciously sensible estimate originating from the office of one Max Arbogast, alias Chic Arbogast, alias Specs Arbogast—a waxy little ectomorph with the glinting eyes of a claim jumper in a Republic western.

When we met at the premises, some inner voice told me I

was face-to-face with someone who would indeed blow up the silver mine while coolies toiled innocently within rather than stand them their wages. My wife, marinated by Arbogast's oily chemistry, was all eagerness, and leaned on me while she succumbed to his Coleridge-like view of what transmogrifications could be effected given the contractor's genius. Our dreams, he assured us, would be realized within six months, and he offered his firstborn as human sacrifice if the budget strayed above this projection. Groveling in the presence of such expertise, I inquired if it were possible that he might give priority to our bedroom and bath so we could move in, thus manumitting us from an overzealous vigorish at the Dilapidado Hotel, our interim fiefdom.

"It's not even a question," Arbogast snapped, producing a contract from a valise stuffed with contracts for every conceivable transaction, from selling a used Cord to enlisting in the Mummers. "Autograph this, and the assorted particulars can be buffed down the line," he said. Thrusting a pen into my hand, he guided it across the dotted lines of a document with large blank sections, whose import, he assured me, would become manifest later by simply holding it over a low flame.

Following apace came a dizzying round of check signings by yours truly, to bind the deal and secure various materials. "Sixty thousand dollars for molly screws seems high," I bleated.

"Sure it is, but then again, you don't want the work held up while we're combing Gotham for one."

Affirming our camaraderie, we all shook hands and went around the corner to Drinks "R" Us, where Arbogast treated all to a magnum of Dom Pérignon, realizing only after the cork had been popped that TWA had mislaid his luggage and that, even as we toasted, his billfold languished in Zanzibar.

*   *   *

THE FIRST TIME I REALIZED we had thrown in our lot with crass bunglers came three months later, when, hours after we had actually taken possession of our under-construction domicile, I attempted to use the stall shower. Heeding our supplication for speed, Arbogast's myrmidons had bashed the original bathroom to protons and hastily fabricated a substitute. Using as their model the lengthy gash in the hull of the *Titanic,* they had transformed the entire bathroom into an undersea kingdom, should my wife or I attempt to turn on the tap. For lagniappe, the pipes had been meticulously calibrated to produce water pressure of such caloric intensity as to reduce any unfortunate beneath the showerhead to the status of lobster thermidor. After my squealing leap through the plate-glass door, I was assured in several Baltic tongues that all would be rectified with the expected arrival of a state-of-the-art plumbing part from Tangier, which would happen the moment certain political exiles could safely be smuggled out of the Casbah.

The bedroom, by contrast, did not quite meet our accelerated target date, owing to an outbreak of dengue fever in Machu Picchu. It seemed, in fact, that no serious work could

begin in our sleeping quarters until we received vital ship-
ments of *wengé* and *bubinga* that had somehow been misde-
livered to a couple in Lapland with the same last name as
ours. Fortunately, a crude pallet on the floor was arranged for
us, under some falling plaster, and after a night of being mar-
tyred by asbestos dust and the sounds of Hurricane Agnes
from a toilet that would not stop flushing, I lapsed at last into
a hypnagogic trance. This was shattered at daybreak by a bat-
talion of craftsmen demolishing a pilaster with pickaxes, to
the tune of "Casey Jones."

When I pointed out that this particular alteration was not
in the original proposal, Arbogast—who had popped in to see
that none of his minions had been shanghaied the prior night
at any of the louche venues they watered at after hours—
explained he had taken it upon himself to install an elaborate
security system.

"Security?" I asked, realizing for the first time that I was
more vulnerable in a brownstone than in our old co-op,
where affable white-haired doormen were lavishly tipped to
take a bullet for the tenants.

"Absotively," he rejoined, wolfing back his matutinal portion of sturgeon direct from Barney Greengrass's numbered
vaults in Geneva. "Any serial killer can just walk into this
place. Maybe you want your throat sliced while you sleep? Or
your main squeeze should get her brains scrambled by some
drifter with a ball-peen hammer and a grudge against society?
And that's after he's had his way with her."

"Do you really think—"

"It's not what *I* think, pilgrim. This town is awash with diabolical mental tinderboxes."

With that, he scribbled in an additional ninety thousand dollars on the estimate, which had waxed to the girth of the Talmud while rivaling it in possible interpretations.

Not wanting to be smirked at by the workers as an easy mark, I insisted that before I could agree to any new costs I would have to peruse the nuances of the risk-reward ratio, a formula that I understood with the same firm grasp I had on quantum mechanics. Since several hot stocks I had invested in recently had vanished without a trace into the Bermuda Triangle, I finally told the work foreman I couldn't dredge up another penny for a burglar-alarm system, but when night fell I froze in bed hearing what I concluded was a homicidal maniac unscrewing the front door. With my heart pounding like the bombing of Dresden, I got Arbogast on the horn and green-lighted the installation of a set of pricey, high-tech Tibetan motion detectors.

.   .   .

AS THE MONTHS PASSED, our completion date, already postponed half a dozen times, kept receding like a six-pack in the desert. Alibis abounded to rival the Arabian Nights. Several plasterers went down with mad cow, and then the boat carrying crates of jade and lapis lazuli to line the nanny's room was sunk off the coast of Auckland by a tsunami; finally, a crucial motorized device needed to elevate the TV from a trunk at the foot of the bed turned out to be hand-fashioned exclusively by elves who worked only by moonlight. The microscopic amount of work that actually took place was shoddy, as I learned in the midst of a sparkling exchange between myself and a Nobel contender in our brand-new study, when the floor buckled, costing the potential laureate his two front teeth and earning me the honor of sponsoring a record settlement.

When I confronted Arbogast with my disenchantment over cost overruns that were challenging the German inflation of the 1920s, he laid it off to my "psychotic demand for change orders."

"Relax, cousin," he said. "If you'll stop your tergiversating, Arbogast and Company will be history in four weeks. My hand to God."

"And not a moment too soon," I fumed. "I can't coexist another second with this infestation from Stonehenge. There's not a scintilla of privacy. Just yesterday, after finally filching some measure of lebensraum, I was about to consummate the sacred act of love with my one and only profiterole when your workers picked me up and moved me so they could hang a sconce."

"See these?" Arbogast said, flashing a smile usually employed by men who are about to commit mail fraud. "They're called Xanax. Dig in—although I wouldn't take more than thirty a day. The side-effect studies have been inconclusive."

That midnight, a susurrus triggered the downstairs motion

detector, causing me to leap directly upright out of bed and remain there like a hovercraft. Convinced that I could make out the sounds of a salivating lycanthrope vaulting up the stairs, I flailed through unpacked cartons in search of some silver object with which to defend the family. Stepping on my glasses in panic, I bolted face-first into a porphyry dolphin Arbogast had imported to complete the maid's bathroom. The blow caused my middle ear to ring like the Arthur Rank logo and rewarded me as well with an unimpeded view of the aurora borealis. I think it was then that the ceiling collapsed on my wife. Apparently the pilaster Arbogast had removed to install the security system had been a supporting member, and a number of cinder blocks had chosen this moment to abdicate.

In the morning I was found curled up on the floor sobbing rhythmically. My spouse had been led away by a stocky woman in a severe suit, wearing a brimmed man's hat, to whom she kept intoning something about always having been dependent on the kindness of strangers. In the end, we sold the house for a song. I can't recall if it was "Am I Blue" or "Brother, Can You Spare a Dime?" I do remember the faces of the building inspectors, however, and the admixture of zeal and dismay with which they enumerated my sundry violations, which they said could be rectified by either further contracting work or accepting a lethal injection. I also have some dim recall of being before a judge who sat glowering like an El Greco cardinal as he mulcted me to the tune of many zeroes, causing my net worth to disappear like the lox at a bris. As for Arbogast, legend has it that, while attempting to hijack an expensive Georgian mantel from someone's fireplace and replace it with a ceramic copy, he managed to get stuck in the flue. Whether he was ultimately consumed by flames I don't know. I tried finding him in Dante's *Inferno,* but I guess they don't update those classics.

ATTENTION GENIUSES: CASH ONLY

❧

J OGGING ALONG FIFTH AVENUE last summer as part
of a fitness program designed to reduce my life ex-
pectancy to that of a nineteenth-century coal miner, I paused
at the outdoor café of the Stanhope Hotel to renovate my flag-
ging respiratory system with a chilled screwdriver. Orange
juice being well up on my prescribed regimen, I quaffed several rounds and upon rising managed to execute a series of
corybantic figures, not unlike the infant Bambi taking his first
steps.

Recalling dimly through a cortex richly marinated by the
Smirnoff people that I had committed to picking up a ration
of goat-cheese buttons and some Holland rusk en route home,
I stumbled numbly into the Metropolitan Museum, mistaking
it for Zabar's. As I lurched down the halls, my head spinning
like a zoetrope, I gradually regained sufficient lucidity to realize that I was bearing witness to an exhibition, Cézanne to
van Gogh: The Collection of Doctor Gachet.

Gachet, I garnered from the wall spiel, was a physician who
treated the likes of Pissarro and van Gogh when these lads

were under the weather after ingesting an unripe frog's leg or belting back too much absinthe. As yet unrecognized and unable to pay a sou, they offered to balance Gachet's books with an oil or pastel in exchange for a house call or a dose of mercury. Gachet's willingness to accept proved clairvoyant, and as I luxuriated in the agglomeration of Renoirs and Cézannes, presumably direct from the walls of his waiting room, I couldn't help imagining myself in a similar situation.

Nov. 1st: *Quelle* good fortune! That I, Dr. Skeezix Feebleman, have received a referral today from none other than Noah Untermensch, a genius among psychoanalysts who specializes in the problems of the creative mind. Untermensch has amassed a prestigious show-business clientele rivaled only by the "Available List" at the William Morris Agency.

"This kid Pepkin's a songwriter," Dr. Untermensch told me over the phone as he greased the skids for a meeting with the prospective patient. "He's Jerry Kern or Cole Porter, but modern-day. Problem is, the kid's awash in debilitating guilt. My best guess? It's a mother thing. Candle his sconce for a while and sluice off some angst. You won't be sorry. I see Tonys, Oscars, Grammys, maybe even a Medal of Freedom."

I asked Untermensch why he wasn't going to treat Pepkin himself. "Plate's full," he snapped, "and all analytic emergencies. Actress whose co-op won't let dogs in, TV weatherman into paddling, plus a producer who can't get a call back from Mike Eisner. Him I placed on suicide watch. Anyway, do your best, and no need to keep me informed about your progress. You get final cut. Ha ha."

Nov. 3rd: Met Murray Pepkin today, and there's no question about it, the man has artist written all over him. Bushy-haired and with eyes like hypnodisks, he is the rarefied man obsessed with his work yet lumbered on all sides by the pygmy demands of food, rent, and two alimonies. As a songwriter, Pepkin appears to be a visionary who chooses to hone his lyrics in a spare room in Queens above Fleisher Brothers Quality Embalming, where he sometimes serves as a makeup consultant. I asked him why he believes he needs analysis, and he confessed that, while the reality is that each note and syllable he pens vibrates with genuine greatness, he feels he's too self-critical. He recognizes his relentless self-destructive choices in women and was recently married to an actress in a relationship based not so much on traditional Western ethics as on Hammurabi's Code. Shortly after, he discovered her in bed with their nutritionist. They quarreled, and she struck Pepkin in the head with his rhyming dictionary, causing him to forget the bridge to "Dry Bones."

When I brought up my fee, Pepkin allowed sheepishly that at the moment he was a bit strapped, having squandered the last of his savings on a duck press. He wondered if we might not arrange some form of installment plan. When I explained that financial obligation was crucial to the treatment itself, he came up with the idea that he might pay me off in songs, pointing out how remunerative it would have been over the years if I alone held the copyright to "Begin the Beguine" or "Send In the Clowns." Not only would the royalties from his sheet music in time swell my personal coffers, but I would be lauded the world over as having nurtured a fledgling tune-smith equal to Gershwin, the Beatles, or Marvin Hamlisch. Having always prided myself on a keen eye for budding talent, and recalling how amply rewarded some old French homeopath named Cachet or Kashay had been writing prescriptions for van Gogh in exchange for an occasional still life to cover the cost of his tongue depressors, I warmed to Pepkin's offer. I also reviewed my own financial obligations, which have puffed recently like a hammered thumb. There was the apartment on Park Avenue, the beach house in Quogue, the two Ferraris, and Foxy Breitbart, an expensive little habit I picked up one night trolling the singles bars, whose skin tones in a thong put a smile on my face that could only be chipped off with a chisel. Add to this a too heavy position in Lebanese guavas and my cash flow seemed a shade coagulated. And yet a voice somewhere within asserted that a flier with this tightly wound mainspring sprawled before me not only might prove an annuity but, should Hollywood one day make his life story, the role of Skeezix Feebleman could just cop Best Supporting Actor.

May 2nd: It has been six months today that I have been treating Murray Pepkin, and though my faith in his genius abides undiminished, I must say I did not realize the amount of work involved. Last week he rang me at 3 A.M. to tell me a long dream in which Rodgers and Hart appeared at his window as parrots and simonized his car. Some days later he paged me at the opera and threatened to take his life if I did not immediately drive to meet him at Umberto's Clam House and hear his idea for a musical based on the Dewey decimal system. I put up with it out of deference to his gifts, which I alone seem to recognize. He has given me, over the last half year, a kilo of songs, some composed hastily on napkins, and although none have as yet found succor at a publishing house, he insists each will in time be a classic. One is a sophisticated bauble called "If You'll Be My Puma in Yuma I'll Be Your Stork in New York." It's best crooned, and is replete with clever double entendres. "Molting Time," by contrast, is a mournful air not unlike the Irish masterpiece "Danny Boy." I agree with Pepkin that only a tenor of genius could do it justice. A beautiful love song Pepkin also guarantees me will eventually top the charts is "My Lips Will Be a Little Late This Year," which boasts the bittersweet lyric "Embrace me, disgrace me, just don't erase me from your Rolodex." For lagniappe in this delightful salmagundi, Pepkin included "Stout-Hearted Mice," which, he assures me, is the kind of patriotic morale builder that, in the event of all-out nuclear war, will glean for me beaucoup jack. Still, a little of the ready for my Herculean efforts would come in handy, what with Foxy, to whom I am engaged, dropping mail-fisted hints regarding a floor-length winter garment in the marten family.

June 10th: I am experiencing some professional problems, which I realize for the "hands on" type of shrink I am is par for the course, and yet to sustain a subdural hematoma the size of a Brunkhorst knockwurst I feel is over the top. The other night, while fast asleep after an arduous day of psychoanalysis, I got a frantic call from Pepkin's wife. At the moment we were speaking she was holding Pepkin at bay with Mace. Apparently she had been critical of his new torch song, "A Side Order of Heartache, Please," suggesting it could be used as a good way to break in their new paper shredder. Realizing what tabloid banner lines top-billing Feebleman could do to a discreet practice should I alert the fuzz, I bolted from my apartment in my underwear and sped possessed over the Fifty-ninth Street Bridge. Arriving at Pepkin's, I found husband and wife feinting around the kitchen table, each trying to gain purchase for a strike. Magda Pepkin gripped a spray can, Pepkin a souvenir he had gotten free on Bat Day at Shea Stadium.

Convinced that a firm tone was needed, I stepped between the two and cleared my throat dramatically just as Pepkin swung the bat at his wife, cracking my head with the sound of a bases-clearing triple. I staggered forward, smiling unmotivatedly at what I imagined to be Alpha Centauri, and recall being taken to the local hospital emergency ward, where I was instantly rushed to the Intensive Apathy Unit.

As for recompense for what one colleague calls "Hippocratic dedication barely discernible from cretinism," I remain on shaky ground. I have accumulated over a hundred songs in lieu of any suggestion of the green and crinkly, and have not had much luck selling them. That not a single music maven I visited could find a molecule of promise in a hot cabaret number like "Make with the Hormones" or the sublime ballad "Early Alzheimer's" has given me fleeting intimations that Pepkin may not be the next Irving Berlin. Still, in his lilting

"Everything's Up to Date at Yonah Schimmel's," which I own and also can't milk a brass farthing from, the line "Knishes and wishes are only for the young" makes me smile with a rueful irony.

Nov. 4th: I have come to the conclusion that Pepkin is a no-talent zombie momser. The center began to spring a leak when I discovered that a series of tax shelters structured to maximize my earnings had begun to strike the IRS as curiously similar to those of Al Capone. Disallowing each one with hand-rubbing glee, the Treasury Department elected to suction my holdings to the tune of eight times my net worth. Unable to inhale when this news descended upon me in the form of a subpoena, I explained to Pepkin that I could no longer afford to treat him on the arm, my furniture being moved out by federal marshals even as we spoke. Touched by this request for some measure of genuine coin of the realm, Pepkin terminated his treatment, and on the advice of some shyster he plays eight ball with sued me for malpractice.

Unable to handle the sudden downsizing and the hardship that accrued when Bergdorf's amputated her charge account, Foxy Breitbart exchanged me even up for an anorexic four-eyed pipsqueak whose computer-chip patent catapulted him, at twenty-five, seven notches above the Sultan of Brunei on a certain list in *Forbes*. Meanwhile, I was left with a trunkful of sheet music with titles like "The Earthworms of Tuscany" and "At the Speleologists' Ball." I tried marketing these tiny white elephants, to no avail, and even checked to see what price they might bring if sold in bulk to a paper-recycling factory. But Pepkin's coup de grâce was yet to come, and come it did, in the person of Wolf Silverglide. Silverglide, a ferret in gabardine, had experienced visions advising him to do a musical reworking of *Lysistrata* called *Not Now, I Have a Headache.* Enlivened by clever modern songs, this Attic chestnut, which happened to be in the public domain, would, in Silverglide's view, turn us all into maharajas. The grapevine clued him in to the fact that I owned a carload of unpublished songs that could be garnered for short money. Dusting off my copyrights at last, I optioned an exaltation of hummable ditties to Silverglide in return for some shares in the enterprise and a vintage black-and-white TV set, and his brainchild lurched into production sporting a complete Murray Pepkin score. The best number was a torch song called "Italics Mine," which boasted the magnificent lyric "You're fine, like rare wine, *I love you* (italics mine)."

The show opened to mixed notices. *The Poultryman's Journal* enjoyed it, as did *Cigar Magazine.* The dailies, along with *Time* and *Newsweek,* were more reserved, forming a consensus best summed up by the critic who called it "a black hole of imbecility." Unable to parse the reviews and come up with any kind of quote ad that didn't appear life-threatening, Silverglide folded his extravaganza like a deck chair and blew town photon-fast, leaving me to deal with the avalanche of plagiary suits that poured in.

It seems that Maestro Pepkin's best music proved upon expert testimony to be a scintilla too proximate to certain trifles like "Body and Soul," "Stardust," and even that old military rouser that begins "From the halls of Montezuma." Meanwhile, I'm in court every day, and although it appears I'm staring off into the middle distance, what I'm really thinking is that if I ever run into the undiscovered van Gogh of ASCAP, I will take one of my last remaining possessions, a straight razor, and cut *both* his ears off (italics mine).

STRUNG OUT

 ❧

I AM GREATLY RELIEVED that the universe is finally ex-
plainable. I was beginning to think it was me. As it turns
out, physics, like a grating relative, has all the answers. The
big bang, black holes, and the primordial soup turn up every
Tuesday in the Science section of the *Times,* and as a result my
grasp of general relativity and quantum mechanics now
equals Einstein's—Einstein Moomjy, that is, the rug seller.
How could I not have known that there are little things the
size of "Planck length" in the universe, which are a millionth
of a billionth of a billionth of a billionth of a centimeter?
Imagine if you dropped one in a dark theater how hard it
would be to find. And how does gravity work? And if it
were to cease suddenly, would certain restaurants still re-
quire a jacket? What I do know about physics is that to
a man standing on the shore, time passes quicker than to a
man on a boat—especially if the man on the boat is with
his wife. The latest miracle of physics is string theory, which
has been heralded as a TOE, or "Theory of Everything." This

may even include the incident of last week herewith described.

I awoke on Friday, and because the universe is expanding it took me longer than usual to find my robe. This made me late leaving for work, and because the concept of up and down is relative, the elevator I got into went to the roof, where it was very difficult to hail a taxi. Please keep in mind that a man on a rocket ship approaching the speed of light would have seemed on time for work—or perhaps even a little early, and certainly better dressed. When I finally got to the office and approached my employer, Mr. Muchnick, to explain the delay, my mass increased the closer I came to him, which he took as a sign of insubordination. There was some rather bitter talk of docking my pay, which, when measured against the speed of light, is very small anyhow. The truth is that compared with the amount of atoms in the Andromeda galaxy I actually earn quite little. I tried to tell this to Mr. Muchnick, who said I was not taking into account that time and space were the same thing. He swore that if that situation should change he would give me a raise. I pointed out that since time and space are the same thing, and it takes three hours to do something that turns out to be less than six inches long, it can't sell for more than five dollars. The one good thing about space being the same as time is that if you travel to the outer reaches of the universe and the voyage takes three thousand earth years, your friends will be dead when you come back, but you will not need Botox.

Back in my office, with the sunlight streaming through the window, I thought to myself that if our great golden star suddenly exploded, this planet would fly out of orbit and hurtle through infinity forever—another good reason to always carry a cell phone. On the other hand, if I could someday go faster than 186,000 miles per second and recapture the light born centuries ago, could I then go back in time to ancient Egypt or imperial Rome? But what would I do there? I hardly knew anybody. It was at this moment that our new secretary, Miss Lola Kelly, walked in. Now, in the debate over whether everything is made up of particles or waves, Miss Kelly is definitely waves. You can tell she's waves every time she walks to the watercooler. Not that she doesn't have good particles, but it's the waves that get her the trinkets from Tiffany's. My wife is more waves than particles, too, it's just that her waves have begun to sag a little. Or maybe the problem is that my wife has too many quarks. The truth is, lately she looks as if she had passed too close to the event horizon of a black hole and some of her—not all of her by any means—was sucked in. It gives her a kind of funny shape, which I'm hoping will be correctable by cold fusion. My advice to anyone has always been to avoid black holes because, once inside, it's extremely hard to climb out and still retain one's ear for music. If, by chance, you do fall all the way through a black hole and emerge from the other side, you'll probably live your entire life over and over but will be too compressed to go out and meet girls.

And so I approached Miss Kelly's gravitational field and

could feel my strings vibrating. All I knew was that I wanted to wrap my weak-gauge bosons around her gluons, slip through a wormhole, and do some quantum tunneling. It was at this point that I was rendered impotent by Heisenberg's uncertainty principle. How could I act if I couldn't determine her exact position and velocity? And what if I should suddenly cause a singularity—that is, a devastating rupture in space-time? They're so noisy. Everyone would look up and I'd be embarrassed in front of Miss Kelly. Ah, but the woman has such good dark energy. Dark energy, though hypothetical, has always been a turn-on for me, especially in a female who has an overbite. I fantasized that if I could only get her into a particle accelerator for five minutes with a bottle of Château Lafite, I'd be standing next to her with our quanta approximating the speed of light and her nucleus colliding with mine. Of course, exactly at this moment I got a piece of antimatter in my eye and had to find a Q-tip to remove it. I had all but lost hope when she turned toward me and spoke.

"I'm sorry," she said. "I was about to order some coffee and Danish, but now I can't seem to remember the Schrödinger equation. Isn't that silly? It's just slipped my mind."

"Evolution of probability waves," I said. "And if you're ordering, I'd love an English muffin with muons and tea."

"My pleasure," she said, smiling coquettishly and curling up into a Calabi-Yau shape. I could feel my coupling constant invade her weak field as I pressed my lips to her wet neutrinos. Apparently I achieved some kind of fission, because the next thing I knew I was picking myself up off the floor with a mouse on my eye the size of a supernova.

I guess physics can explain everything except the softer sex, although I told my wife I got the shiner because the universe was contracting, not expanding, and I just wasn't paying attention.

ABOVE THE LAW,
BELOW THE BOX SPRINGS

❧

WILTON'S CREEK lies at the center of the Great Plains, north of Shepherd's Grove, to the left of Dobb's Point, and just above the bluffs that form Planck's constant. The land is arable and is found primarily on the ground. Once a year, the swirling winds from the Kinna Hurrah rip through the open fields, lifting farmers from their work and depositing them hundreds of miles to the south, where they often resettle and open boutiques. On a gray Tuesday morning in June, Comfort Tobias, the Washburns' housekeeper, entered the Washburn home, as she has done each day for the past seventeen years. The fact that she was fired nine years ago has not stopped her coming to clean, and the Washburns value her more than ever since terminating her wages. Before working for the Washburns, Tobias was a horse whisperer at a ranch in Texas, but she suffered a nervous breakdown when a horse whispered back. "What stunned me most," she recalls, "was that he knew my Social Security number."

When Comfort Tobias entered the Washburn house that Tuesday, the family was off on vacation. (They had stowed away on a cruise ship to the Greek islands, and although they'd hidden in barrels and done without food or water for three weeks, the Washburns did manage to sneak out on deck at 3 A.M. each night to play shuffleboard.) Tobias went upstairs to change a lightbulb.

"Mrs. Washburn liked her lightbulbs changed every Tuesday and Friday, whether they needed it or not," she explained. "She loved fresh lightbulbs. The linens we did once a year."

The minute the housekeeper entered the master bedroom, she knew something was amiss. Then she saw it—she couldn't believe her eyes! Someone had been at the mattress and had cut off the tag that reads, "It is a violation of law to remove this tag, except by the consumer." Tobias shuddered. Her legs buckled and she felt sick. Something told her to look in the children's rooms, and sure enough, there, too, the tags had been removed from the mattresses. Now her blood froze as she saw a large shadow loom ominously across the wall. Her heart pounded and she wanted to scream. Then she recognized the shadow as her own and, resolving to diet, phoned the police.

"I've never seen anything like it," Chief Homer Pugh said. "Things like this just don't go on in Wilton's Creek. Sure, one time somebody broke into the local bakery and sucked the jelly out of the doughnuts, but the third time it happened we had marksmen up on the roof and we shot him in the act."

"Why? Why?" sobbed Bonnie Beale, a neighbor of the Washburns'. "So senseless, so cruel. What kind of world are we living in when someone other than the consumer cuts off the mattress tags?"

"Before this," Maude Figgins, the local schoolteacher, said, "when I'd go out I could always leave my mattresses home. Now whenever I leave my house, whether it's to go shopping or out to dinner, I'm taking all my mattresses along."

. . . .

AT MIDNIGHT THAT EVENING, along the road to Amarillo, Texas, two people drove at high speed in a red Ford with fake license plates that looked real from a distance but on closer inspection were clearly made of marzipan. The driver had a tattoo on his right forearm that read, "Peace, Love, Decency." When he rolled up his left sleeve another tattoo appeared: "Printing Error—Disregard My Right Forearm."

Next to him was a young blond woman who might have been considered beautiful if she had not been a dead ringer for Abe Vigoda. The driver, Beau Stubbs, had recently escaped from San Quentin, where he had been incarcerated for littering. Stubbs was convicted of dropping a Snickers wrapper on the street, and the judge, claiming that he had shown no remorse, sentenced him to two consecutive life terms.

The woman, Doxy Nash, had been married to an undertaker and worked beside him. Stubbs had entered their funeral parlor one day, just to browse. Smitten, he tried to make flirtatious conversation with her, but she was too busy cremating someone. It wasn't long before Stubbs and Doxy Nash began having a secret affair, although soon she found out about it. Her undertaker husband, Wilbur, liked Stubbs and offered to bury him gratis if he would agree to have it done that day. Stubbs knocked him unconscious and ran away with his wife but not before substituting a rubber blow-up doll in her place. One evening, after three of the happiest years of Wilbur Nash's life, he became suspicious when he asked his wife for more chicken and she suddenly popped and flew around the room in ever-diminishing circles, coming to rest on the carpet.

· · ·

HOMER PUGH STANDS FIVE-EIGHT in his stocking feet, which he keeps in a large duffel bag along with his actual feet. Pugh has been a policeman as far back as he can remember. His father was a notorious bank robber, and the only way Pugh could get to spend time with him was to apprehend him. Pugh arrested his father on nine occasions; he values their conversations, although many took place while the two men were exchanging gunfire.

I asked Pugh what he made of the situation.

"My theory?" Pugh said. " 'Two drifters, off to see the world . . .' " Soon he was singing "Moon River" while his wife, Ann, served drinks, and I was given a fifty-six-dollar tab. Just then the phone rang, and Pugh pounced on it. The voice at the other end came across the room with deep resonance.

"Homer?"

"Willard," Pugh said. It was Willard Boggs—Trooper Boggs of the Amarillo state police. The state police in Amarillo are a crackerjack group, and members not only must be physically impressive but must pass a rigorous written exam. Boggs had failed the written test twice, first being unable to explicate Wittgenstein to the desk sergeant's satisfaction, then mistranslating Ovid. It was a mark of his dedication that Boggs received tutoring, and his final thesis on Jane Austen remains a classic among the motorcycle police who patrol Amarillo's highways.

"We got our eye on a couple," he told Chief Pugh. "Very suspicious behavior."

"Like what?" Pugh asked, lighting yet another cigarette. Pugh is aware of the health hazards of smoking and so uses only chocolate cigarettes. When he lights the tips, the chocolate melts on his trousers, giving him enormous cleaning bills on a policeman's salary.

"Couple came into a fancy restaurant here," Boggs continued. "Ordered a big barbecue dinner, wine, all the trimmings. Ran up a whopping check and tried paying with mattress tags."

"Pick 'em up," Pugh said. "Bring 'em in, but don't tell anybody what the charge is. Say they fit the description of two people we want for questioning about fondling a hen."

The state law on removing the tag of a mattress that does not belong to you goes back to the early 1900s, when Asa Chones engaged in a quarrel with his neighbor over a pig that had wandered into the neighbor's yard. The two men fought over possession of the pig for several hours, until Chones realized that it was not a pig at all but his wife. The matter was adjudicated by the town elders, who ruled that Chones's wife's features were sufficiently porcine to justify the mistake. In a fit of rage, Chones entered the neighbor's home that night and tore off all the man's mattress tags. He was apprehended and stood trial. The mattress minus the tag, reasoned the court verdict, "insults the integrity of the stuffing."

At first Nash and Stubbs maintained their innocence, claiming to be a ventriloquist and puppet. By 2 A.M. both suspects had begun to crack under Pugh's relentless interrogation, which was cleverly done in French, a language they did not know, and hence could not easily lie in. Finally, Stubbs confessed.

*   *   *

"WE PULLED UP in front of the Washburn house in the moonlight," he said. "We knew the front door was always left open, but we broke in just to keep in practice. Doxy turned all the Washburn family photos to the wall so there wouldn't be any witnesses. I'd heard about the Washburns in prison from Wade Mullaway, a serial killer who dismembered his victims and ate them. He'd worked as a chef for the Washburns but was let go when they found a nose in their soufflé. I knew it was not only illegal but a crime against God to remove tags from mattresses where I was not the consumer, but I kept hearing this voice telling me to do it. If I'm not mistaken, it was Walter Cronkite. I cut the Washburns' tag, Doxy did the kids' mattresses. I was sweating—the room was blurry—my whole childhood passed before my eyes, then another kid's childhood, and finally the childhood of the Nizam of Hyderabad."

At the trial Stubbs chose to act as his own lawyer, but a conflict over his fee led to ill feelings. I visited Beau Stubbs on Death Row, where numerous appeals kept him from the gallows for a decade, in which time he used prison to learn a trade and became a highly skilled airline pilot. I was present when the final sentence was carried out. A great sum of money was paid to Stubbs by Nike for the television rights, allowing the company to put its logo on the front of his black hood. Whether the death penalty acts as a deterrent remains questionable, although studies show that the odds of criminals committing another crime drops by almost half after their execution.

Thus Ate Zarathustra

∽

There's nothing like the discovery of an unknown work by a great thinker to set the intellectual community atwitter and cause academics to dart about like those things one sees when looking at a drop of water under a microscope. On a recent trip to Heidelberg to procure some rare nineteenth-century dueling scars, I happened upon just such a treasure. Who would have thought that *Friedrich Nietzsche's Diet Book* existed? While its authenticity might appear to be a soupçon dicey to the niggling, most who have studied the work agree that no other Western thinker has come so close to reconciling Plato with Pritikin. Selections follow.

· · ·

Fat itself is a substance or essence of a substance or mode of that essence. The big problem sets in when it accumulates on your hips. Among the pre-Socratics, it was Zeno who held that weight was an illusion and that no matter how much a man ate he would always be only half as fat as the man who never does push-ups. The quest for an ideal body obsessed the

Athenians, and in a lost play by Aeschylus, Clytemnestra breaks her vow never to snack between meals and tears out her eyes when she realizes she no longer fits into her bathing suit.

It took the mind of Aristotle to put the weight problem into scientific terms, and in an early fragment of the *Ethics* he states that the circumference of any man is equal to his girth multiplied by pi. This sufficed until the Middle Ages, when Aquinas translated a number of menus into Latin and the first really good oyster bars opened. Dining out was still frowned upon by the Church, and valet parking was a venal sin.

As we know, for centuries Rome regarded the Open Hot Turkey Sandwich as the height of licentiousness; many sandwiches were forced to stay closed and only reopened after the Reformation. Fourteenth-century religious paintings first depicted scenes of damnation in which the overweight wandered Hell, condemned to salads and yogurt. The Spaniards were particularly cruel, and during the Inquisition a man could be put to death for stuffing an avocado with crabmeat.

No philosopher came close to solving the problem of guilt and weight until Descartes divided mind and body in two, so that the body could gorge itself while the mind thought, Who cares? It's not me. The great question of philosophy remains: If life is meaningless, what can be done about alphabet soup? It was Leibniz who first said that fat consisted of monads. Leibniz dieted and exercised but never did get rid of his monads—at least, not the ones that adhered to his thighs. Spinoza, on the other hand, dined sparingly because he believed that God existed in everything and it's intimidating to wolf down a knish if you think you're ladling mustard onto the First Cause of All Things.

Is there a relationship between a healthy regimen and creative genius? We need only look at the composer Richard Wagner and see what he puts away. French fries, grilled cheese, nachos—Christ, there's no limit to the man's appetite, and yet his music is sublime. Cosima, his wife, goes pretty good, too, but at least she runs every day. In a scene cut from the Ring cycle, Siegfried decides to dine out with the Rhine maidens and in heroic fashion consumes an ox, two dozen fowl, several wheels of cheese, and fifteen kegs of beer. Then the check comes and he's short. The point here is that in life one is entitled to a side dish of either coleslaw or potato salad, and the choice must be made in terror, with the knowledge that not only is our time on earth limited but most kitchens close at ten.

The existential catastrophe for Schopenhauer was not so much eating as munching. Schopenhauer railed against the aimless nibbling of peanuts and potato chips while one engaged in other activities. Once munching has begun, Schopenhauer held, the human will cannot resist further munching, and the result is a universe with crumbs over everything. No less misguided was Kant, who proposed that we order lunch in such a manner that if everybody ordered the same thing, the world would function in a moral way. The problem Kant didn't foresee is that if everyone orders the same dish, there will be squabbling in the kitchen over who gets the last branzino. "Order like you are ordering for every human being on earth," Kant advises; but what if the man next to you doesn't eat guacamole? In the end, of course, there are no moral foods—unless we count soft-boiled eggs.

. . .

TO SUM UP: apart from my own Beyond Good and Evil Flapjacks and Will to Power Salad Dressing, of the truly great recipes that have changed Western ideas Hegel's Chicken Pot Pie was the first to employ leftovers with meaningful political implications. Spinoza's Stir-Fried Shrimp and Vegetables can be enjoyed by atheists and agnostics alike, while a little-known recipe of Hobbes's for Barbecued Baby Back Ribs remains an intellectual conundrum. The great thing about the Nietzsche Diet is that once the pounds are shed they stay off—which is not the case with Kant's "Tractatus on Starches."

BREAKFAST

Orange juice

2 strips bacon

Profiteroles

Baked clams

Toast

Herbal tea

The juice of the orange is the very being of the orange made manifest, and by this I mean its true nature, and that which gives it its "orangeness" and keeps it from tasting like, say, a

poached salmon or grits. To the devout, the notion of anything but cereal for breakfast produces anxiety and dread, but
with the death of God anything is permitted, and profiteroles
and clams may be eaten at will, and even buffalo wings.

LUNCH

1 bowl spaghetti, with tomato and basil

White bread

Mashed potatoes

Sacher torte

The powerful will always lunch on rich foods, well seasoned
with heavy sauces, while the weak peck away at wheat germ
and tofu, convinced that their suffering will earn them a re-
ward in an afterlife where grilled lamb chops are all the rage.
But if the afterlife is, as I assert, an eternal recurrence of this
life, then the meek must dine in perpetuity on low carbs and
broiled chicken with the skin removed.

DINNER

Steak or sausages

Hash-brown potatoes

Lobster thermidor

Ice cream with whipped cream or layer cake

This is a meal for the Superman. Let those who are riddled
with angst over high triglycerides and trans fats eat to please
their pastor or nutritionist, but the Superman knows that
marbleized meat and creamy cheeses with rich desserts and,

oh, yes, lots of fried stuff is what Dionysus would eat—if it weren't for his reflux problem.

APHORISMS

Epistemology renders dieting moot. If nothing exists except in my mind, not only can I order anything, the service will be impeccable.

Man is the only creature who ever stiffs a waiter.

Surprise Rocks Disney Trial

❧

THE WALT DISNEY COMPANY shareholder suit over the severance package paid to departing president Michael Ovitz was jolted today by the testimony of an unexpected witness, who was questioned by counsel for the entertainment giant.

COUNSEL   Will the witness please state his name.

WITNESS   Mickey Mouse.

C   Please tell the court your occupation.

W   Animated rodent.

C   Were you friendly with Michael Eisner?

W   I wouldn't say friendly—we had dinner together a number of times. Once he and his wife had Minnie and me to their house.

C   Did you ever discuss business with him?

w   I was present at a breakfast between Mr. Eisner, Roy Disney, Pluto, and Goofy.

c   Where was this breakfast?

w   At the Beverly Hills Hotel.

c   Were there any other witnesses?

w   Steven Spielberg stopped at our table to say hello . . . oh, and Daffy Duck.

c   You're acquainted with Daffy Duck?

w   Daffy Duck and I had met at a dinner at Sue Mengers's home some months back and had become friendly.

c   I take it Mr. Eisner did not approve of this relationship with Daffy Duck?

w   We quarreled over it several times.

c   What finally happened?

w   I eventually stopped seeing Daffy when he became a Scientologist.

c   I direct you back to the breakfast. Do you recall what was discussed?

w   Mr. Eisner said that he planned to hire Michael Ovitz, the head of CAA.

c   How did you feel about that?

w   I was surprised, but Pluto took the news harder. He seemed despondent.

c   Why despondent?

w   He was worried because Mr. Ovitz had a much closer relationship with Goofy, and Pluto felt his screen time might be reduced.

c   So you were aware of a "special relationship" between Mr. Ovitz and Goofy?

w   I knew that when Mr. Ovitz was an agent he had courted Goofy, and if I'm not mistaken, the two shared a house together in Aspen.

c   Did there come a time when they became closer?

w   Mr. Ovitz stood by Goofy when he was busted in Malibu.

c   Is it true Goofy had a drug problem?

w   He was addicted to Percodan.

c   How long had that been going on?

w   Goofy went on painkillers after a flop he took in a cartoon. He parachuted off the Empire State Building with an umbrella and hurt his back.

c   And?

w   Mr. Ovitz was responsible for getting Goofy into the Betty Ford Center.

c   Did you ever tell Mr. Eisner of your apprehensions over his plan to hire Mr. Ovitz?

w   Minnie and I discussed it. We knew they'd clash.

c   Did you bring it up with anyone besides your wife?

w   Dumbo, Bambi—I really can't remember. Oh, yes—Jiminy Cricket, one time at Barbra Streisand's house. She threw a party for Jiminy when he bought his place in Trancas.

c   And was anything concluded?

w   Dumbo felt that Donald Duck should talk to Mr. Eisner about our concerns because Mr. Eisner always seemed to listen to Donald. As he put it, Donald was "one of the deepest ducks he'd ever met." The two spent a lot of time together in Donald's pond.

c   And was the relationship reciprocal?

w   Oh, yes. Donald lived at Mr. Eisner's home for six months when he and Daisy Duck were separated. Donald had been having an affair with Petunia Pig, Porky's girlfriend. It was a no-no at Disney to socialize with creatures from a competing studio, but in Donald's case Mr. Eisner chose to look the other way, which upset the shareholders.

c   This was the affair you referred to in your deposition?

w   Yes. My memory's hazy on this, but I think Donald was introduced to Petunia Pig at the home of Jeffrey Katzenberg.

c   You were present?

w   Yes. Myself, Tom Cruise, Tom Hanks, Jack Nicholson. I believe Sean Penn, Wile E. Coyote, the Road Runner—

c   Tom and Jerry?

w   No, they were at EST that weekend.

c   It was six months later when Mr. Katzenberg and Mr. Eisner became involved in a lawsuit. Do you recall those details?

w   It had to do with Mr. Eisner promising stock options to Bugs Bunny if he would come to work at Disney.

c   And did Bugs?

w   No. Bugs was his own man. At that time he wanted to take a year off to write a novel.

c   Getting back to the party—do you recall what happened next?

w   Yes. Donald Duck got drunk and made a pass at Nicole Kidman. It was extremely embarrassing because at the time she and Tom Cruise were still married. Donald was rather hostile to Tom, I recall, and felt Tom was being offered all the roles he wanted. I recall Mr. Eisner at that party taking Donald outside to calm him down.

c   Do you recall what happened next?

w   On the lawn of Mr. Katzenberg's house Donald met Petunia Pig. He found her very beautiful and very exciting and I know they liked a lot of the same music groups. And Donald always had a problem with anger management. He had been on Prozac for years because he'd become convinced his career had tanked and soon he would wind up on a Cantonese menu. Despite Mr. Eisner's advice, Donald began seeing Porky's girlfriend on the sly.

c   To the best of your knowledge, how long did the affair continue?

w   For about a year. Petunia told Donald she couldn't keep seeing him because she'd fallen deeply in love with Warren Beatty and he with her. If you recall, Warren took her to the Cannes Film Festival.

c   Did there come a time when Daisy Duck threw Donald out?

w   Yes, and Mr. Eisner took him in and let him live at his house till Donald and Daisy finally agreed that they'd live together again but have an open relationship sexually.

c   So, to the best of your recollection, did anyone at all ever tell Mr. Eisner it might not be a good idea to hire Mr. Ovitz?

w   The night of the Academy Awards I brought it up to Pinocchio, but he didn't want to get involved.

c   And so you're saying neither Pinocchio nor anyone else warned Mr. Eisner that he and Mr. Ovitz might be an incompatible match.

w   To the best of my knowledge, that's correct.

c   And when the job didn't work out the subject came up of Mr. Ovitz's severance package—the $140 million payment? Did Mr. Ovitz ever feel it was excessive?

w   I just know that Jiminy Cricket was often perched on Mr. Ovitz's shoulder and advised him to always let his conscience be his guide.

c   And?

w   The rest is history.

c   Your witness.

PINCHUCK'S LAW

❧

TWENTY YEARS in the homicide division of the NYPD and, brother, you've seen everything. Like when some Wall Street broker juliennes his little petit four over who gets to work the channel changer, or this lovesick rabbi decides to end it all by salting his beard with anthrax and inhaling. That's why when someone reported a dead body on Riverside Drive at Eighty-third with no bullet holes, no stab wounds, and no signs of struggle I didn't freak to some film-noir conclusion but put it down to one of the thousand natural shocks the Bard claims the flesh is heir to but don't ask me which one.

When another stiff turned up in SoHo two days later, though, also without the least trace of foul play, and a third likewise in Central Park, I got out the Dexedrine and told the immortal beloved I'd be working late for a while.

"It's amazing," my partner, Mike Sweeney, said as he strung the usual yellow bunting around the crime scene. Mike is a bear of a man who could easily pass for a bear, and has in fact been contacted by zoos to fill in when the real bear was

155

ill. "The tabloids are saying it's a serial killer. Naturally, the serial killers are claiming bias and that they're always the first ones accused when three or more victims are killed the same way. They'd like the number raised to six."

"I'll level with you, Mike, I've never seen anything like this one—and you know I'm the guy who collared the Astrology Killer." The Astrology Killer was a vicious maniac who liked to sneak up and bash people's heads in while they were yodeling. He was tough to nab because there was so much sympathy for him.

I told Mike to call me if he came up with any sexy clues and I beat it down to the morgue to ask Sam Dogstatter, our coroner, about poison. Sam and I go way back to when he was a young coroner starting out and used to perform autopsies at weddings and sweet sixteens for cigarette money.

"At first I thought it might be a tiny dart," Sam said. "I tried to check out everybody in New York City who owned a blow gun, but the task was insurmountable. No one realizes half the town's got one of those six-foot Jívaro jobs and most citizens have carrying permits."

I brought up the possibility of the Amanita mushroom, which can kill without leaving any trace, but Sam shot it down. "There was only one health-food store that sold really deadly mushrooms, but it stopped years ago when it turned out they weren't organically grown."

I thanked Sam and put in a call to Lou Watson, who was excited because he'd gotten a very good set of fingerprints at the crime scene, which he instantly traded to another precinct for a rare set of Enrico Caruso's that were quite valuable. Lou said the lab had come up with a hair. They had also come up with a bald spot. The hair unfortunately matched an eight-year-old kid's and the bald spot was traced to a row of nine men in the front row of a girlie show, who all had airtight alibis.

Down at headquarters, I chatted with Ben Rogers, my mentor and the man who solved the Yuppie Restaurant Murder Case, where the victims were shot and then lightly dusted with lime and fresh mint. Ben had waited till the killer ran out of fresh mint and was forced to use chopped walnuts, which were traceable by their serial numbers.

"Tell me about the victims," I said. "Did they have any enemies?"

"Sure, they had enemies," Ben said, "but their enemies were all at Mar-A-Lago, in Palm Beach. There was a big Enemies Convention and practically every enemy on the East Coast attended."

I had just left Ben to grab a sandwich when I got word that a hot-off-the-griddle stiff had turned up in a Dumpster on East Seventy-second Street. This time the pristine corpse was Ricky Weems, a young actor who specialized in sensitive rebels and was the star of the TV medical soap opera *When a Mole Darkens.* Only this time a homeless lady caught the action. Wanda Bushkin, who'd once slept every night in a carton on the Lower East Side, had recently moved to a carton on Park Avenue. At first, she worried that she wouldn't get board approval, but when her net worth was shown to be above four dollars and thirty cents she was accepted at the more desirable box.

Bushkin couldn't sleep on the night in question and caught sight of a man who drove up in a red Hummer, tossed a body, and sped away. At first, she didn't want to get involved because she had once identified a criminal who then broke off his engagement to her. This time, she described the suspect to our sketch artist, Howard Inchcape, but Inchcape, in a fit of temperament, refused to do the picture unless the suspect would come in and sit for it.

I was trying to reason with Inchcape when my mind suddenly twigged on B. J. Sygmnd, the psychic. Sygmnd was a poor Austrian who'd lost all the vowels in his name in a boating accident. In 1993, I had used Sygmnd to find a cat burglar, whom he rather miraculously picked out from almost a hundred strays. I watched now while he poked around at the victim's belongings and then went into some kind of trance. His eyeballs widened and he started to speak but the voice that came from him was that of Toshiro Mifune. He said the man I was looking for employed Novocain and worked with drills on molars and bicuspids, and he might even be able to pinpoint the profession but he needed a Ouija board.

A quick computer check corroborated that all the victims were patients of the same DDS, and I knew I'd hit pay dirt. Anesthetizing myself with four fingers of Johnnie Walker, I used a Swiss Army knife to pry out the silver amalgam in lower seven, and the next morning sat openmouthed while Dr. Paul W. Pinchuck worked on my cavity.

"This won't take long," he said. "Although if you have a little time I should also do the tooth next to it. I'm surprised it hasn't given you any trouble. You're not missing anything outside today, anyhow. Can you believe this weather? April set a record for rainfall. It's this global-warming thing. Because too many people use air conditioners. I don't need one. Where we live you sleep with the window open even in the hottest weather. I have a good metabolism that way. My wife, too. Both our bodies adjust well. Because we're very careful about what we eat. No marbleized meat, not too much dairy—plus I exercise. I prefer the treadmill. Miriam likes the StairMaster. And we very much enjoy swimming. We have a house out in Sagaponack. Miriam and I usually begin taking the weekends, the start of April, out in the Hamptons. We love Sagaponack. There's people if you want to socialize but you can also keep to yourself. I'm not a big social person. We like to read, mostly, and she does origami. We used to have a place in Tappan. There's a few different ways to go but I usually take I-95. It's a half hour. We prefer the beach, though. We just put in a new roof. I couldn't believe the estimate. My God, those contractors get you every which way. Look, it's like anything else—you get what you pay for. I tell my kids there are no bargains in this life. There's no free lunch. We have three boys. Seth will be bar mitzvahed in June."

I began to feel myself gasping for air as Pinchuck's drill cut through my enamel and I fought the onset of Cheyne-Stokes breathing. I sensed my vital signs were ebbing, and I knew I was in trouble when my life began to pass before my eyes and my father was being played by Dame Edna.

Four days later I awoke in the intensive-care unit at Columbia-Presbyterian.

"Thank God you're made of iron," Mike Sweeney said, leaning over my bed.

"What happened?" I queried.

"You were very lucky," Mike said. "Just as you lost consciousness, a Mrs. Fay Noseworthy burst into Pinchuck's office with a dental emergency. She was an FWI: Flossing While Intoxicated. Apparently it caused her temporary crowns to slip out and she swallowed them. When you hit the floor at Pinchuck's, she began screaming. Pinchuck panicked and made a run for it. Fortunately, our SWAT team got there just in time."

"Pinchuck ran? But he seemed just like any regular dentist. He worked on my teeth and chatted."

"Right now, you get some rest," Mike said, flashing his Mona Lisa smile, which Sotheby's had claimed was a forgery. "I'll explain it all when you're up on your feet."

In case you're wondering where this little homicide tale goes, keep watching the back pages for news out of Albany, where the legislature will be taking up the bill that will lead to Pinchuck's Law, which makes it a felony for any dentist to endanger the life of a patient by relentless conversation or by saying anything other than "Open wide" or "Please rinse" without a prior court order.

Woody Allen's prolific career as a comedian, writer, and filmmaker has now spanned more than five decades. He writes frequently for *The New Yorker* and is the author of *Without Feathers, Getting Even,* and *Side Effects,* among other books.

ABOUT THE TYPE

This book was set in Sabon, a typeface designed
by the well-known German typographer Jan
Tschichold (1902–74). Sabon's design is based
upon the original letter forms of Claude Gara-
mond and was created specifically to be used for
three sources: foundry type for hand composi-
tion, Linotype, and Monotype. Tschichold named
his typeface for the famous Frankfurt type-
founder Jacques Sabon, who died in 1580.